YOUNG GUMS

10 9 8 7 6 5 4

Ebury Press, an imprint of Ebury Publishing,
20 Vauxhall Bridge Road,
London, SW1V 2SA

Ebury Press is part of the Penguin Random House group of companies
whose addresses can be found at global.penguinrandomhouse.com

First published by Ebury Press in 2018

www.penguin.co.uk

A CIP catalogue record for this book is available from the British Library

Design: Clare Skeats
Photography: Haarala Hamilton
Food stylists: Kitty Coles and Frankie Unsworth
Prop Stylist: Grace Poulter

ISBN: 9781785038105

Colour reproduction by Altaimage Ltd, London
Printed and bound in Italy by L.E.G.O. S.p.A.

YOUNG GUMS

Baby food with attitude

Beth Bentley

Contents

Nutritionist's foreword

Dr. Emma Derbyshire RNutr PhD

What a breath of fresh air for new parents. This fresh, clever and much-needed book gives modern parents bags of reliable know-how for making creative, nutritious and yet affordable baby meals from scratch, every day.

This book has a real edge above other baby cookbooks. The nutritional advice is solid, up-to-the-minute and relatable, and the recipes are refreshingly simple and easy to achieve. Stand-out dishes for me include the 'one-family-one-meal' recipes: the curries, stews, chillies and sharing breakfasts such as flavoured pancakes and porridges. Eating together as a family is a fantastic habit to form – not only does it introduce your child to the social aspects of mealtimes, but eating the same thing as a parent can really help a baby accept and enjoy new tastes.

Beth's other baby-feeding philosophies also make good sense to me as an expert in this field. Her 'best of both' approach to the finger food or spoon-feeding question is sensible, and finding ways to combine both feeding methods in the same dish (like the Magic Fish Fingers with crushed pea dip) is very creative. Going big and bold with flavour when cooking for babies is a wonderful rule of thumb. It's important to stoke a baby's natural curiosity by exposing them to as many different food flavours, ingredients, textures and cuisines as possible, as early as possible. And I like the idea of parents using their parental judgement to introduce new foods at a pace that they feel is right for their child. That said, Beth has written a handy guide full of tips and hints to guide your intuition week-by week and month-by-month – see p.32.

I am pleased to see that the core messages in Young Gums are so well aligned with the globally recognised World Health Organization infant feeding recommendations. In line with latest evidence, I am also happy to see the use of unrefined whole grains, whole fruits and vegetables (fibre-rich skin and all – great move!), a wide range of protein sources, and the absence of any refined sugars and refined carbohydrates. Special mention on that last point must also go to the first birthday party celebration table – what a feast, and not a grain of refined sugar in sight. I also love the parent-boosting snacks tucked away at the back of the book. As a parent of a young child myself I am very much on board with the idea of nourishing ourselves as we learn to nourish our babies (I'm also on board with the One Hand Cooking … I'm sure all new parents can relate to this!).

Beth is a refreshing – and welcome – new voice in weaning. She makes this potentially confusing stage of new parenthood feel wonderfully simple, and presents cooking for your baby as an adventure rather than a chore (regardless of how sharp your culinary skills are). You can tell how much fun she has in her own kitchen and I very much hope her enthusiasm inspires yours.

Emma Derbyshire heads up Nutritional Insight Ltd, a consultancy to food, healthcare and Government organisations. She has expertise in maternal and child nutrition. She is also the co-founder of LittleFoodie.Org – an organisation providing expert advice on early year's nutrition.

Introduction

Hi. Welcome to Young Gums, the modern parent's guide to raising a happy, healthy eater.

This collection of healthy, creative and fun recipes will guide you from the very start of your weaning journey right through to your baby's first birthday, and beyond. He or she will encounter a huge range of tasty, nourishing, interesting dishes that I hope will help establish a happy lifelong relationship with good, whole, real food.

This is a baby food cookbook unlike any other. You'll see ingredients and flavours you might not expect. And you'll find no rigid month-by-month stages to tick off (although there is a helpful weaning timeline on p.32). Everything here is safe from the very start of weaning and each recipe is flexible enough to evolve in texture, serving style and portion size as your baby develops. And best of all, everything is quick, easy and inexpensive. Some of the dishes are so easy you can make them without even putting your baby down. Welcome to the world of #OneHandCooking.

All nutritional advice has been approved by infant nutrition expert and clinical nutritionist, Dr. Emma Derbyshire, and is in line with up-to-date World Health Organization advice on weaning. As well as Emma, while writing this book I read and spoke to psychologists, dieticians, and food historians, as well as grandmothers and great-grandmothers from different food cultures. Every recipe has been triple-tested for ease, accuracy and tastiness by real parents of real weaning babies – members of the thousands-strong Young Gums online community. Ideas and feedback from all over the world have helped hone these recipes. It takes a village!

The parents in my network also helped me build the *Baby Feeding FAQs* section at p.19. I asked them what they wished they'd known at the start of weaning, and figured out simple, clear answers to the questions that came up again and again. I hope our collective experiences can help you as you begin your weaning journey.

Speaking of us parents, at the end of the book you'll find a special selection of recipes just for you. It's easy to overlook nourishing ourselves as we focus on nourishing our babies, and these nutrient-packed snacks have the power to pick you up and keep you going no matter *how* badly you slept last night.

In closing, know this: if you choose to cook for your baby, you're in good company. In fact you're part of a growing global tribe, and I don't just mean the Young Gums community. Sales of manufactured baby food are in decline in many countries as more and more Millennial parents choose to cook for their babies.

I hope your baby likes these recipes as much as mine does, and I hope you enjoy reading this book half as much as I enjoyed writing it.

Ok let's get started. We've got hungry babies to feed.

Beth x
London Fields, Spring 2018

Join the community:
www.instagram.com/young_gums
www.younggums.com

The story behind this book

Some of my earliest memories are of helping my parents and grandparents in the kitchen. I'm from a foodie family and enjoy cooking so the idea of weaning my baby was exciting. It was going to be one LOL after another. The messy-face photos! Cute egg in the hair! Oh, the videos we'd make.

But a couple of weeks before she started solids, I walked with Baby B down the baby food aisle in the supermarket for the first time. And suddenly my excitement melted away, replaced by disappointment with an edge of frustration. So many highly processed foods: vegetable-flavoured maize puffs, flavoured and fortified juice drinks, rice snacks sweetened with concentrated fruit syrup, baby biscuits made with refined flour and artificial flavourings. Almost everything was puréed, and almost everything contained cooked fruit...even savoury things like stews and pasta sauces. And though the aisle was packed, the range of flavours, ingredients and textures seemed pretty narrow and repetitive.

If this was the 'normal' modern Western approach to baby weaning, I wasn't sure I liked it.

That supermarket trip changed my life. It led me to setting up an online content platform that brings together thousands of like-minded mums, dads, grandparents and childcare professionals; to meeting inspiring experts in food, nutrition and parenting; and to writing this book, which contains everything I wish I'd known when I was sitting where you are right now.

Young Gums began at my kitchen table in East London, last year, the morning my baby started solids. I set up an Instagram account and posted a couple of pictures, using the captions to share my feelings about approaching the task of teaching a baby to eat against the backdrop of our chaotic and highly processed 21st-century food landscape. How daunting I found the responsibility, how difficult it was to find nutritious baby food in the shops. Over the coming days I shared my first recipes. Within the week, hundreds of parents had found the account. I connected with nutritionists, academics, food writers, local restaurateurs, food industry experts and even an investigative journalist. I'd struck on something other people thought was important, too.

Establishing and maintaining good eating habits in our children has to be one of the trickiest responsibilities facing a 21st- century parent. It's widely held that the modern Western childhood diet is too often high in the wrong things, low in the right things, and detached from where food comes from, or what season it is. Children like what they know, and in a world where processed, artificially flavoured foods are abundant, that's of course what many of them know.

What kids eat early in life matters. Diet-related health conditions are rising steeply in the very young: type 2 diabetes, fatty liver disease, obesity and more. Sugar-decayed milk teeth are surgically extracted at a rate of 500 cases a week in the UK. Dietary deficiencies from the history books are returning as some kids' childhoods are spent overfed yet undernourished. It's not a social 'class' thing, far from it. The stats are too widespread. Jamie Oliver famously said in his 2010 TED talk *Teach Every Child About Food*, 'Children exposed to unhealthy, highly processed foods are at risk of living a shorter and less healthy life than their parents.' A shocking statement that's not nice for any parent to hear, but it focused my mind when I heard it. I'm not here to scaremonger – quite the opposite. I want feeding our babies to be fun and creative and joyful, not a source of anxiety.

The good news? There are so many things we can do, from the very start of weaning, to help our babies grow up familiar with a wide range of real, unprocessed food.

One thing is to go big, early, with flavour. In her book *First Bite: How We Learn to Eat*, food theorist Bee Wilson refers to evidence stating that between (roughly) learning to sit up and learning to crawl, a baby is psychologically more receptive to new tastes than they're ever likely to be again. This 'flavour window' doesn't abruptly shut, she says, but does narrow as the child enters toddlerhood, making it more difficult to accept unfamiliar tastes. So let's go big and broad, early. Wilson also suggests that babies

I've spent a lot of time #OneHandCooking and my baby loves to see what's happening in the pots and pans.

can on some level 'remember' flavour profiles from babyhood that stay with them as they grow up and make their own decisions about what to eat.

Another is to eat together with our babies. Psychologists say time spent at the table is invaluable for babies as they learn the social side of eating – the way people share food, eat with cutlery, take turns talking … and don't rub banana in their hair. Where you can, eat the same food as them – many dishes in this book are meals the whole family can share: tagines, stews, curries, pancakes, and more.

And a third is to familiarise your baby with what real, raw food looks like. Let them watch you peel potatoes or crack eggs. Point out different ingredients when you go food shopping and let them see what you are doing when you are cooking.

An interesting place to learn to eat

Where we live is an important part of the Young Gums story. London Fields, in East London, isn't just the backdrop to my Instagram blog. It's also my ongoing source of recipe inspiration. One of the oldest and most cosmopolitan parts of the city, London Fields is now home to a vibrant and creative food scene.

An incredible food market arrives every Saturday. We join queues for Israeli street-food, Mexican burritos, Basque tapas, or bowls of messy-but-worth-it laksa, dhal, gumbo, and chowder. Chilli-scattered bao, steaming dim sum, oil-drizzled arancini. Ancient grain galettes oozing with French cheese. Herb-studded flatbreads oozing with Greek cheese. North African tagines, South African biltong. Brazilian stews, Hawaiian poke. Snacks spiked with pestos, tapenades; squeezes of lime. Then comes gelato, granita, raw cheesecake, spiced popcorn, bliss balls and chia pudding. Real, fresh, tasty food. A world of it in one street.

That kind of food inspiration can't help but rub off on a mama and you'll see echoes of this inspiration throughout my recipes.

Mindful baby feeding ... huh?

Mindful feeding is how I sum up Young Gums when asked. It means taking a moment to consider the meal you're about to offer – what's in it, where it came from, and the effect it'll have on your baby's body. 'Mindfulness' is a trendy concept we've heard a lot recently, but there's nothing flash-in-the-pan about this approach. It harks back to simpler times, before baby food became so industrialised.

My mindful baby feeding mantras

Don't feed your baby anything your great-grandmother wouldn't recognise

The words of world renowned food theorist Michael Pollan have been ringing in my ears while writing this book. In his bestselling book about the modern adult diet, *Food Rules: An Eater's Manual*, he said, 'Don't eat anything your great-grandmother wouldn't recognise as food'. Of course, my own great-grandmothers wouldn't be familiar with some of my ingredients (avocados and blueberries weren't especially abundant in 1930s rural Ireland, nor along the rugged Welsh coast...), but I know they'd see eye-to-eye with me on my simple, whole food choices and traditional cooking techniques.

It's not all on you

Pioneering American baby-feeding academic and author, Ellyn Satter, is widely quoted by infant nutritionists – even governments – for her division-of-labour concept: 'The parent is responsible for what, when, where. The child is responsible for how much and whether.' It may feel like a strange idea to expect your little person to take responsibility for anything, but it's very liberating. Provide good food at appropriate times, and trust your baby to eat what they need.

Stoke your baby's natural curiosity about food

The flavours in this book might seem bigger than you expected. There may be ingredients you wouldn't have considered to be *baby food*. But weaning babies can safely eat much more widely than we might think. Going big with flavour now could stand your baby in good stead later in life.

Leave anxiety at the (kitchen) door

Every recipe here is easily achievable no matter how confident you are in the kitchen (and no matter how little sleep you had last night). Ingredients lists are short – easy-to-find, basic things. And methods are quick – no fancy equipment, short cooking times.

Let your baby watch...from your hip

Necessity is the mother of invention. When hunger struck, my baby would never be put down. She had to hug. If I was going to get any cooking done, it was going to have to be with her on my hip... and #OneHandCooking was born.

Baby-feeding FAQs

As every new parent knows, there's a *lot* of conflicting advice around weaning. Start with purées, bringing in chunkier textures once the baby's learned to swallow. No, start with finger food so they learn to chew before swallowing. Encourage the baby to become familiar with a few foods to begin with, establishing favourites they get excited about. No, offer plenty of variety and don't let the diet become repetitive…that'll make it much harder to introduce new foods. Offer the baby their own bowl of food so they learn to be independent, eating what they feel like and stopping when they're full. No, hold the bowl yourself and feed them slowly with a spoon. Let them refuse a food, it's part of the journey. Don't let them refuse a food, keep offering it – ten times. No, eight. No, sixteen times should do it. A full tummy will help them sleep through the night. A full tummy won't help them sleep through the night.

To bring some order to the chaos I polled my online community for the BIG weaning questions, and talked them through with some experts – a GP, an infant nutritionist, and a child psychologist.

Weaning: when to start?

Let's start with the big one. The World Health Organization's guidelines have remained unchanged since 2003: for around the first six months of life, a baby will receive all required nutrition from breastmilk or correctly made-up formula. The view is that additional food is unnecessary and early weaning may even have a detrimental effect on the immature digestive system.

WHO's three signs your baby is ready to eat

1. Baby can sit up independently, holding head steady.
2. Baby has hand-eye coordination to look at an object, pick it up and put it in their mouth.
3. 'Tongue-thrust' reflex has relaxed. Babies are born with an evolutionary protection mechanism … the tongue automatically pushes things out of the mouth in case they're dangerous. This reflex relaxes when the baby's ready to learn to chew and swallow, but it can be tricky to assess. Touch a spoonful of food to the baby's bottom lip. Either the tongue will immediately push it away or the baby will open their mouth. It might take several attempts over a few days, but you'll know it when you see it. Gagging and spitting out is normal. It tends to be loud (and messy), as the baby coughs, spits and repositions the food in their mouth. However, choking can be near-silent, so ensure your baby is always with an adult while eating and drinking and understand how to handle choking. Your doctor or healthcare practitioner can demonstrate.

WHO states that these behaviours are normal developmental stages and not indicators that it's time to wean (unless accompanied by all three of the above): chewing fists, reaching for something a parent is eating, waking more often at night, sudden cluster-feeding (if breastfeeding) or seeking larger/more frequent bottle feeds.

WHO says 'around six months' as some show readiness a little ahead, and others after. I like the advice of American infant nutrition expert, Ellyn Satter: 'Go by what your baby can do, not by their age.'

The other reason that around six months is considered the optimum time for solid foods is to do with a key mineral: iron. Babies are born with only about 6 months' supply and after this must find it in their diet. Modern commercial weaning foods, like baby rice, are often chemically fortified with iron for this reason. Or you can skip the packets and cook with foods naturally iron-rich like lean red meat, green vegetables and pulses. I'll show you how.

It's not advised to offer food before 4 months of age as the kidneys and digestive system aren't considered mature enough, and neither is it recommended to wait very much longer than 6 months of age because at this point the growing baby's birth stores of iron deplete rapidly. If your baby was premature the guidelines may apply differently, so seek your doctor's advice.

What are the best early foods to give? What do little babies like to eat?

The short answer is to offer as broad a range of foods as possible, that are as natural and unprocessed as possible.

Physiologically, a weaning baby can safely eat and enjoy an astonishing variety of foods. There's evidence to suggest babies of this age are more open and receptive to flavour than they will ever be again in their lives (particularly flavours that are bitter or sour). Many grow more cautious in their preferences as they approach toddlerhood, but certainly to begin with you may be surprised just how many foods your baby shows interest in.

Should I avoid shop-bought baby food?

No. I would never be so unrealistic to suggest busy, tired new parents avoid all commercially produced baby foods. Some varieties are of course more nutritious than others, but in my opinion pre-made baby foods absolutely have a role in busy family life. What I do suggest is that we try to put industrially produced baby food in its place: convenience food that is handy in a bind, but not an everyday staple of our babies' diets.

We can reconfigure what we think of as baby food ... when I'm in a mad rush I'll run to the corner shop for a banana and plain yoghurt, low-mess fruit like blueberries or an apple I can break into pieces.

The thing that focused my mind on learning to cook quick daily baby meals was this: one day I was reading a baby food label in the supermarket and noticed a symbol stating the product was safe to sit on the shelf for up to 18 months. Looking at my six month old, I realised the food in the jar could easily be older than the baby...indeed, the ingredients could have been picked and cooked before this kid was even conceived.

Purées or finger foods?

The big news in baby feeding over the past decade or so has been baby-led weaning: giving your baby fist-sized pieces of appropriate foods from day one of weaning, rather than mashing, mixing or puréeing foods and feeding via spoon.

This philosophy liberated many parents, making mealtimes a bit more freestyle and giving the baby more control to express their curiosity and make decisions about what to eat, in what order. It can be crazy-messy of course … but I'm a big fan.

However there are brilliant things about spoon-feeding, too. It can be a special kind of bonding experience for baby and parent: the eye contact, the non-verbal communication. And practically, getting a little food into a hungry baby's mouth quite quickly and efficiently can mean the child doesn't become frustrated trying to feed themselves and may enjoy the mealtime feeling calmer and happier.

In this book and on my social feeds, I take a best-of-both philosophy. You'll find lots of hand-held finger food for your baby to explore, and lots of dishes a parent can help the baby to eat by spoon. Sometimes you'll find both modes of feeding in the same meal… a dippy pea purée with a crunchy fish-finger, for example, or a creamy hummus with a cold, crunchy cucumber stick. Almost any meal lends itself to 'best of both' … just mash or whizz some of it, and leave some pieces intact.

Can I make these recipes from day one of weaning?

Almost. There's no physiological reason why the dishes in this book couldn't be fed from the very first day. However, it's very wise to ring-fence the first couple of weeks as your time to check for possible food allergies or reactions. Foods regarded as potential allergens should be introduced one by one first and then built into meals so that reactions can easily be identified. Plus, the baby will eat such tiny portions at this stage that it's often easier to stick to simple one-ingredient meals (see p.32 for suggestions).

How will I know if my baby's allergic to a food?

Allergies can take various forms and cause different reactions. Sometimes an allergy is immediately obvious, sometimes it can take a while to present. While diagnoses of food and non-food allergies and intolerances are generally on the rise across the developed world, severe food reactions are thankfully extremely rare and often run in families, so ask your relatives before you begin weaning. The most common allergenic foods for babies are dairy, egg (egg reaction often disappears later in babyhood, and it is more often the white than the yolk that causes the reaction), soya, wheat and nuts. Peanuts cause more reactions than any other nut (although it's actually a legume rather than a nut) followed by various types of nuts that grow on trees. Nuts are so incredibly nutritious that, unless you feel that your baby is likely to have a reaction, latest advice is that these foods should be introduced from around 6 months. The easiest way is with smooth pure nut butters.

How much food should I offer and how often?

A general rule of thumb for portion sizes and number of meals per day, based on the latest World Health Organization advice:

6–7 months: 1-2 meals a day, meal size up to 4 teaspoons

7–9 months: 3 meals a day, meal size 2–4 tablespoons

9–12 months: 3 meals a day, meal size 4–6 tablespoons, plus a snack if needed mid-morning/mid-afternoon

If the baby's looking for more, offer it. If your baby doesn't want this much, don't be concerned. Some babies don't (mine didn't!). Offer in a relaxed way a few times and if the baby's not interested, end the mealtime. Appetite can fluctuate from one day to the next with growth spurts, teething, changes of routine, or tiredness. Create a relaxed eating environment. A baby shouldn't feel they've upset or pleased a parent by eating or not. And one thing a baby knows is when he or she is full, so let them learn to recognise the full-tummy feeling and not always coax them to 'eat one last bit'.

Allergy UK's advice on spotting a food allergy in a baby

'Mild allergy' symptoms: seek medical attention if baby is distressed or if symptoms worsen rather than subside (call the family doctor)

- *Flushed face, redness/itchy rash around mouth, spreading to face and body*
- *Mild swelling of lips, eyes or whole face*
- *Runny or blocked nose, sneezing, watering eyes*
- *Vomiting, upset tummy and diarrhoea after eating*
- *Itching/scratching at mouth or throat*

'Severe allergy' symptoms: extremely rare but require emergency medical attention (call an ambulance without hesitation, nobody will think you're being over-cautious)

- *Wheezing or apparent difficulty breathing*
- *Swelling of tongue or throat*
- *Loss of consciousness*

Try not to feel disheartened if the baby refuses something you thought they'd love. Even if absolutely nothing goes into your baby's mouth, which will probably happen to you – or if most of it ends up on the floor, which will definitely happen – the baby (and you) will have learned something new every mealtime.

Is there an ideal mealtime to start with?

No, it's up to you to begin whenever you feel will work best in your family's routine. Some parents swear by beginning with lunch, when the baby's well-rested after a mid-morning nap. Others like to start with early evening dinnertime as there's a better chance of gathering the family to eat together. Some like to begin the day offering their baby some breakfast (that's what I did), and others find their baby is still full from their morning milk. Whichever you prefer, stick with it for the first couple of weeks and be roughly consistent with the time of the day eating happens.

Once your baby is used to a mealtime, try adding another. Snacks can be added in and around meals and milk feeds, as you like. If family life sometimes makes it difficult to stick to a pattern, don't worry. One will emerge eventually.

What does a balanced baby diet look like?

To support their growth and development, babies need to find a broad spectrum of nutrients in their diets. In a nutshell they need:

Three macronutrients

Carbohydrate fuel for the body's engine room. We'll be cooking with a variety of healthy carbs from unrefined grains, vegetables and fruits.

Protein building blocks of growth and repair. 'Complete' protein is found in meat, fish, dairy and eggs, which contain all nine amino acids. 'Incomplete' protein contains some of the nine, and is found in plant sources such as lentils, beans, chickpeas, nuts, nut butters, seeds and seed butters (like tahini).

Fat the engine's lubricator. Not only does it perform many functions (health of skin, joints, brain and blood vessels), fat in the diet enables the baby's body to absorb fat-soluble vitamins. We'll be cooking with foods that contain fats from animal sources (dairy, meat, fish) and from plant sources (coconut milk and oil, avocado, nut or seed butters, plant oils like olive/vegetable oil).

Many micronutrients

The human body holds at least 50 micronutrients – some are vitamins, some are minerals. Many are known as 'essential' because the body cannot generate them itself and must find them in food. Not every micronutrient is present in every recipe but with some mixing and matching your baby will rack up a broad spectrum.

Should I decrease the amount of milk my baby has now he/she's eating food?

No. During early weaning food is as well as milk, not instead. The frequency and volume of milk feeds will naturally decrease over weeks and months as the baby becomes familiar with eating and begins to receive more nutrition from their food, but there's no rush. It's advised to keep going with your normal milk feeding sequence until your baby shows signs it's time to start dialing down their daily volume of milk. Maybe they turn down some of their bottle or start seeking the breast less often. Follow your instinct. Sometimes a baby's appetite for milk will shoot back up, for example if poorly or teething. Check with your doctor if you're unsure.

The British NHS' guidance suggests that at about six months old a baby roughly needs 600-900ml milk daily, 400-500ml daily by their first birthday, and 350ml per day by 18 months, remaining steady until at least the second birthday. Your baby might be different, these are rough guides. If you're breastfeeding without pumping, it's impossible to measure volumes with accuracy, but you will notice the duration and frequency of feeds decreases over time.

In the early stages, some parents offer their baby a short milk feed before a meal to take the edge off their hunger. Once weaning's established, swap for water and keep milk for other times of day.

Should I offer my baby water to drink now that I'm offering solid foods?

When a baby is 6 months old, you can start offering sips of tap or filtered water from a sippy cup or small open cup alongside meals. There are no minimum/maximum volumes of water to offer a weaning baby, but I find putting a cup on the table with every meal reminds me to give my baby the opportunity to sip.

Why shouldn't babies eat sugary foods?

Humans are hardwired by evolution to enjoy sweet tastes. It's thought to be a throwback to ancient times: sugar's easy for the body to process into quick energy for hunting or gathering.

In the modern diet sugar comes in two forms: naturally occurring fruit sugar and refined sugar. Sugars in fruit are a perfectly healthy part of a balanced baby diet because fruit brings with it useful fibre, vitamins, minerals, water and antioxidant compounds.

Refined sugar, such as those found in bags of sugar, brings with it little nourishment. Worse, it's thought to inhibit the body's ability to absorb certain nutrition from other foods. Sugar is addictive because the immediate 'high' is rewarding for the brain. But the ensuing 'low' brings tiredness and irritability. A small child who eats a lot of sugar can become psychologically and physiologically attached to sweet foods, a habit that's tough to break.

Can my baby have cow's milk now?

The WHO's advice is yes, from six months old all dairy is now safe as an ingredient in meals (milk, unsalted butter and cheese, unsweetened yoghurt, and any other pasturised dairy items your family likes to eat). But cow's milk is not recommended as a drink until the first birthday.

Should I go organic?

One of the most contentious issues in modern baby feeding, this is a question I'm yet to find a straight answer to. I buy organic meat, eggs and dairy, and upgrade fresh produce where I can. Why? Firstly, organic land is free from chemical pesticides and fertilisers. That simpler, more old-fashioned approach appeals to me. Secondly, there's a theory (that's quite controversial) suggesting organic food is more nutritious. Nutrient levels in soil are diminishing by the decade (food writer Michael Pollan suggests you'd have to eat three apples today to achieve the nutrient-load of one 1940 apple) and, having no chemical fertilisers, an organic plant has to root deeper to find nutrient-rich soil, resulting, the theory goes, in fruit and vegetables that are higher in vitamins and minerals.

Weaning timeline

My aim with this timeline is to provide enough structure and guidance to help you feel well-informed, but not so much that your parental intuition is stifled. This isn't a rigid week-by-week, clock-watching feeding schedule. This book is based on the latest nutritional evidence available at the time of writing, and every recipe is safe from 6 months, so you're free to open the book anywhere you like and cook whatever catches your eye.

SIX MONTHS:
WEEK ONE

Put your baby in the highchair and play, sing, read or talk – make it a nice place to be. Show them their new bib, bowl, plate and spoon. Pick a regular mealtime and stick to it roughly each day (see p.26 for advice on choosing).

The first week or so is your time to check for any food reactions, so stick to simple one-ingredient meals and watch your baby for allergy symptoms listed on p.25. A meal will be perhaps just two teaspoons or a single small hand-held piece of food, and it'll be slow-going. But don't be anxious about how much is eaten. Bring your baby to the table for as many family meals as possible this week, even if he/she isn't hungry. They'll learn a lot by watching.

Good tiny one-ingredient meals (mashed or in fist-sized pieces)

Avocado
Banana
Steamed carrot or sweet potato
Steamed apple
Soft, ripe pear
Strawberries, raspberries
Peach
Smooth nut butter (watching carefully for reactions)
Unsweetened Greek yoghurt (or soya yoghurt)
Porridge oats simmered in your baby's usual milk or water
Hard-boiled egg, mashed

SIX MONTHS: WEEK TWO TO FOUR

Continue the 'one-ingredient meal' approach, bringing in different foods so that you expose your baby to a range by the end the fortnight. If your baby seems comfortable, with no reactions, go ahead and start combining ingredients into recipes. If your baby's a little disinterested, continue as you are for another week or two. Every baby is different and there's no rush.

Easy-to-eat very first recipes

Baby bircher (see p.48)
Chia pudding (see p.54)
Baby smoothie bowls (see p.46)
Superbaby superporridge (see p.42)
No-roast chicken pot-roast (see p.97)
Brazilian baked jackets (see p.114)
One-ingredient ice cream (see p.139)
Baby burrito bowl (see p.100)
Malaysian coconut fish curry (see p.132)

SEVEN MONTHS

Start mixing simple ingredients together and begin to experiment with simple recipes. Keep an eye out for any emerging favourite foods (you'll know … wait for the leg-waggling and table-bashing!). There's no need to alter milk feed patterns yet: food's still as well, not instead, of milk. Consider adding a second mealtime into the day, or a snack for when you're out and about.

Portable pram snacks

Raw vegetables
Baby bliss balls (see p.144)
Oatcake crackers (see p.87)
Courgette + cheese muffins (see p.88)

EIGHT MONTHS

Your baby may have a few teeth by now, so you could consider some of the more challenging food textures (or mash/blend your cooking less smoothly). If sore gums attack, return to softer, easy dishes.

Recipes for babies learning about biting

Magic fish fingers (see p.107)
Lamb kofta lollipops (see p.120)
Jammy dodgers (see p.155)
Baby bliss balls (see p.144)

Recipes for babies with sore gums

One-ingredient ice cream (see p.139)
Yoghurt bark (see p.160)
Homemade teething biscuits (see p.79)

NINE MONTHS

Your baby might be mobile by now: crawling, sliding, pulling up on the furniture. This developmental leap can affect appetite, so if you notice your baby is more enthusiastic at the table, increase portion sizes. Consider adding in a third mealtime or an extra snack. Continue pushing the boundaries with flavour.

Recipes for adventurous, curious eaters

Baby green curry (see p.108)
Mini Moroccan tagine (see p.125)
Baby burrito bowl (see p.100)

TEN TO ELEVEN MONTHS

Your baby is probably interested enough in food now to eat three times a day, plus perhaps a snack. You may notice the baby's appetite for milk waning slightly as food takes a more central role in their diet, or you might not yet. This age is a great time to encourage independent use of a spoon, and maybe help the baby master using a small open cup – just take the spout off their sippy cup. Your baby might now really enjoy interesting-looking meals with different textures and colours.

Recipes for babies interested in texture and colour

Baby hummus (and the traffic light game) (see p.68)
Melting middle meatballs, on spaghetti or as slider burgers (see p.110)
PJ pancakes in stacks (see p.56)

BY YOUR BABY'S FIRST BIRTHDAY

Hopefully you've had chance to cook all sorts of things and have a baby who's experienced a wide range of tastes. You're probably an expert in #onehandcooking by now. And there's a birthday approaching! While weaning is of course not 'done' yet (your baby will spend at least another year learning about food and mealitimes), you've come a long way and there is plenty to celebrate. Check out my guide to creating a healthy celebration table – and cake – for your baby's first birthday (see p.166).

Congratulations.
You did it. Together.

Weaning store cupboard

Having a bunch of versatile staples at hand means you can put together all sorts of quick baby meals whenever hunger strikes. What's good to have in?

Most of the items here are inexpensive, simple foods in their most basic form. I've tried to be economical with the costly ingredients (e.g. alternative flours, nut butters, coconut oil), suggesting multiple ways of using each in the recipes. Of course our babies deserve the best we can give, but cash can be tighter than usual during early parenthood.

Cupboard staples

Dry goods oats, flour (I cook with wholewheat, spelt or buckwheat flour as they're more nutritious than white flour)

Pulses/pastas/rice wholewheat pasta, brown basmati rice, red and green lentils

Oils olive oil, coconut oil

Spices turmeric, cumin, cinnamon, nutmeg, vanilla extract, oregano, salt-free vegetable bouillon powder

Tins coconut milk (full-fat, without chemical thickeners/emulsifiers), chickpeas, black beans, plum tomatoes, sardines, tuna

Nuts/nut butters ground almonds, smooth almond butter

Store-cupboard fruits/seeds dates, desiccated coconut, chia seeds

The kind of weaning-friendly fresh produce I use in my recipes

Fruit bananas, blueberries, pears, orchard variety apples; soft fruits like peaches or nectarines, strawberries, raspberries and plums; soft tropical fruits like kiwi and mango

Vegetables carrots, sweet potatoes, butternut squash, spinach, avocados, cucumbers, tomatoes, broccoli, courgettes, garlic

For the fridge unsalted butter, Cheddar cheese, whole milk, plain yoghurt

For the freezer peas, berries, cherries, sliced-up bananas

Weaning equipment

With so many weaning products on offer, it's hard to know what's useful and what isn't. Less-is-more, I think. Here are a few things I find handy for the recipes in this book.

For cooking

Small, simple food blender one that is easy to wash (I use a NutriBullet because it's good with small quantities of food, but a cheap stick blender is also great)

Pan-top vegetable steamer or create your own by placing a metal sieve over a pan of simmering water with a close-fitting pan lid on top

Small saucepan

Vegetable grater

Vegetable peeler

Mini muffin tin

Small ice-lolly moulds

Small pots with lids (for pram snacks and for saving leftovers)

For feeding

Small bowls and a plate made of bamboo fibre or BPA-free plastic – easy to wash and unbreakable (a bowl with a rubber sucker on the bottom is the dream … unflingable).

Rubber-tipped spoons this is softer on teething gums than a metal teaspoon and won't heat up on contact with warm food

Bibs with sleeves or silicone bibs with a pouch-front to catch dropped food

Muslin cloths remember all those muslin cloths from the newborn days? They're about to come in handy again. Tie diagonally to create an emergency bib. If you're out and about without a high chair, spread a muslin on your lap before sitting your baby there to eat…save your jeans from food splatters. Cut them into squares and dampen under the tap: washable baby wipes for messy mealtimes

What you don't need (for my recipes)

Weighing scales we use standard teaspoons, tablespoons and teacups to measure … who has time to fiddle with scales?

Microwave I don't have one

Rolling pin use a wine bottle

I return over and over again to a handful of quick, well-balanced recipes that are easy enough for my foggy, morning brain to remember.

Breakfast time

Mornings begin so much sooner than they used to, don't they? Previously unimaginably early starts are the new normal. Bleary-eyed blanket cuddles and fuzzy head rubs after a muddled night's rest. Open the curtains, blink at the dawn. Get the kettle on.

Mornings are not my time for experimenting. Instead, I stick to proven favourites. Made from simple staples, these are pretty basic – although nutritionally they're anything but.

But first ... we need to talk about OATS

Oats. Hardly an ingredient in the land more economical or versatile. Don't be fooled by the quiet oat. They're too shy to say it themselves so I'll say it for them: oats are way more special than they look. Dense with slow-release carbohydrate energy, easily digested fibre, and minerals like magnesium and potassium, they're a brilliant way to start your baby's day. Gluten-free oats are easy to find in supermarkets if your baby has a sensitivity.

Superbaby superporridge

Oats at the ready. Porridge might be simple, but with this formula it'll never be boring. The combinations are endless and it's so easy you can do it with your eyes closed and a baby on your hip. Handy at 6am. I'm sure you don't need me to talk you through making porridge. You made a human. But just in case ...

1. Choose a milk
Expressed breast, formula, cow's, lactose-free cow's, coconut, almond, brown rice milk (check the packaging of nut and plant milks to ensure you're buying unsweetened – sugar creeps into these by stealth) … or water.

2. Choose a fruit
Banana, mango, blueberry, strawberry, raspberry, cherry, grated apple or pear, ripe plum.

3. Pick a superpower
Chia seeds; ground almonds; ground-up pumpkin seeds, linseed, sunflower seeds; a sprinkle of cinnamon, turmeric, cardamom, nutmeg; smooth nut butter ... almond, cashew, peanut (avoid if you have a concern about a possible nut allergy in your baby).

Two of my favourite versions are on the next pages, but here are a few to get you rolling:

Tropical island: coconut milk + mashed banana + chia seeds

Sweet and spicy chai: water + mashed mango + pinch of ground cinnamon + pinch of ground cardamom

Nuts 'n' berries: almond milk + blueberries + smooth almond butter

British summertime: cow's milk + mashed strawberries + ground-up sunflower seeds

Monkey nuts: cow's milk + mashed banana + peanut butter

FOR 1 ADULT + 1 LITTLE ONE

WHAT DO I DO?

- Put 4 tbsp porridge oats into a small pan and pour in 8 tbsp of your chosen liquid. Heat gently and keep stirring.
- Once the liquid has been absorbed, add 8 more tbsp of milk (or water) and repeat. Constant stirring prevents the porridge from sticking and burning, and also creates that famous creamy texture.
- Repeat the liquid – adding another 8 tbsp (to make 24 tbsp in total), and you'll soon be looking at a lovely pan of porridge that's ready to pimp with your chosen additions.

Grandma's apple pie porridge

Traditional in the blustery British autumn, an apple pie is a hug in a bowl. Here I take inspiration from my grandmother's apple pie recipe to create a breakfast that evokes all sorts of happy memories.

FOR 1 ADULT + 1 LITTLE ONE

WHAT DO I NEED?

2 small apples (orchard varieties like Braeburn, Jonagold or a sweet Cox work best), peeled and grated
2 teacups of cold water
4 tbsp porridge oats
¼ tsp ground cinnamon and/or nutmeg
drop of vanilla extract (optional)

WHAT DO I DO?

- Put the apples in a small pan with the teacups of cold water. Bring the pan to a simmer. Meanwhile put the oats into your blender and whizz to fine powder.
- Tip the porridge oats into the simmering pan of fruit and stir continually for 5–6 minutes. The apple will break down as it cooks and the porridge oats will turn everything creamy and gorgeous.
- Serve with a little cinnamon and/or nutmeg. A drop of vanilla will also really dial up the apple pie vibes.

Raspberry macaron porridge

Coconuts and raspberries get on famously. Together they tick nearly every nutrition box: good fats, dietary fibre, almost the entire vitamin spectrum. And this flavour combo is my favourite. It takes me back to a snowy afternoon in Paris on the riverbank with B's dad and a pretty box of raspberry and coconut macarons. We stopped on a bench and, mid-macaron, he asked me to marry him. Good times.

FOR 1 ADULT + 1 LITTLE ONE

WHAT DO I NEED?

4 tbsp porridge oats
½ a 400ml can coconut milk
6 squished fresh/frozen raspberries

WHAT DO I DO?

- Put the porridge oats and coconut milk into a small pan. Put the pan on a gentle heat and stir continuously as the milk warms. After 5–6 minutes the oats will be soft and creamy.
- Just before serving, add the squished raspberries and stir. Pink porridge!

Baby smoothie bowls

I feel a fraud being all cheffy because really this is hardly a recipe at all … the blender does the work for you, whizzing up a nutrient-thick smoothie that's nutrient dense and easy to digest. And, of course, majorly Instagram-able. Creativity, tick. And it's only 7am.

FOR 1 ADULT + 1 LITTLE ONE

WHAT DO I NEED?

6 tbsp coconut milk or plain yoghurt
4 tsp oats
½ banana

Your choice of additions

2 tsp smooth nut butter
few berries (blueberries, raspberries, strawberries, blackberries – fresh/frozen)
slices of any ripe fruit (mango, peach, nectarine, plum, soft pear)
sweet spices (a little ground cinnamon, nutmeg, cardamom, star anise)
artful sprinkle of chia seeds, milled linseed, ground pumpkin seeds or ground almonds

WHAT DO I DO?

• Tip your ingredients into your blender and whizz until smooth. Pour into a few bowls and decorate with your chosen additions, then serve by spoon.
• Make it interactive by serving it with dunkable fist-sized pieces of fresh banana, ripe pear, peach/nectarine, plum or mango.

I can't open my Instagram most mornings without seeing loads of pretty little smoothie bowls staring back at me.

Cherry Bakewell smoothie bowl

As well as being packed with vitamin C, powerful antioxidant compounds, fibre and calcium, the cherry is a natural source of melatonin: a natural chemical that makes us feel relaxed and drowsy. The ground almonds and almond milk bring good fats, protein, vitamin E and magnesium. And the banana? Easily digested carbohydrate energy plus the mineral potassium, which supports heart and muscle function.

If it's a hot day you can use banana slices straight from the freezer to achieve a semifreddo ice cream-like texture.

FOR 1 ADULT + 1 LITTLE ONE

WHAT DO I NEED?

12–16 cherries, stoned
1 banana
2 tsp oats
2 tbsp ground almonds, plus extra to sprinkle
8 tbsp almond milk

WHAT DO I DO?

Put the cherries into your blender with the banana, oats, ground almonds and almond milk. Whizz and serve in little bowls with a sprinkle of ground almonds to decorate.

Baby bircher (overnight oats)

Another big hitter on the hipster breakfast circuit. It also makes a smashing baby breakfast. But where did it come from? Was it invented by the hipsters? Nope, a Swiss doctor was given soaked oats for breakfast one morning on an Alpine hiking holiday early last century. He was so impressed that he named the dish after himself and hiked off home to serve it to the patients in his hospital, who thrived eating the nutrient-packed dish. Cool.

FOR 1 ADULT + 1 LITTLE ONE

WHAT DO I NEED?

4 tbsp oats
12 tbsp milk, or your baby's usual milk
2 apples, peeled and finely grated
¼ tsp ground cinnamon

Your choice of additions

a few drops of vanilla extract
large handful of chopped blueberries/raspberries

WHAT DO I DO?

- The night before, combine everything in a small bowl or jar. Cover with a lid or plate and tuck it up in the fridge. Go to bed (HURRAH).
- By the time you wake up … well, maybe the second or third time you wake up … when it's *actually the morning* … the oats will have swelled to create a soft, spoonable texture that's easy for a weaning baby to eat. Even if they're low on teeth.

Throw together these ingredients before you go to bed and you'll wake up to a feast, no cooking required.

Huevos rancheros (Mexican eggs)

B's dad and I first had this on hols in Tulum and ever since it's been on heavy rotation in our house. Not an obvious weaning meal, but our version's packed with baby-friendly ingredients and the texture's a dream for anyone without a full set of gnashers. Tomatoes and mild onion bring much needed dietary fibre. Smoked paprika and cumin bring vitamins A, E and B6, iron, zinc, calcium, selenium, magnesium and various phytochemicals with powerful antioxidant effects. And the egg is one of nature's cleverest foods, containing almost everything a growing baby needs.

FOR 2 ADULTS + 2 LITTLE ONES

WHAT DO I NEED?

splash of olive oil
2 red or white onions, finely diced
¼ tsp ground cumin
¼ tsp smoked paprika
1 × 400ml can of plum tomatoes
4 eggs

Toppings

grated Cheddar
4 tsp plain yoghurt

WHAT DO I DO?

- Heat a slug of olive oil in a saucepan over a medium-low heat and add the onion. When it's soft and translucent, add the spices and tomatoes. Bash up the tomatoes as you stir. Allow the mixture to stew for a few minutes on a gentle heat, stirring regularly.
- Now for the magic bit. Press your spoon into the mixture to create four hollows. Crack the eggs into the hollows and watch them slowly cook. Allow the yolk and white to solidify, then gently transfer into bowls.
- Fork-mash your egg and sauce to the right texture for your baby and top with a little grated cheese and a teaspoon of yoghurt. If your baby's anything like mine, he or she is about to go totally, totally Mexico.

Sunrise power baby protein bowl

Bowl food is one of the biggest food trends in recent years and protein's also having a bit of a moment – every time I nip to the supermarket I see snazzy protein yoghurts, bars and balls. Protein's the nutrient mainly responsible for growth and cell repair, very useful for these fast-growing babies of ours, and here we're getting it from Greek yoghurt. We first made protein bowls on holiday when B was 9 months old (and hungry from all that crawling). The only equipment in our Airbnb was a fork, so I had to improvise.

FOR 1 ADULT + 1 LITTLE ONE

WHAT DO I NEED?

4 tbsp plain thick Greek yoghurt
8 tsp chopped ripe soft fruits (peach, nectarine, berries, plum)
small handful of almonds, finely shredded
small handful of sunflower seeds, finely shredded
1 tsp chia seeds

WHAT DO I DO?

- Split the yoghurt between bowls, smoothing the surfaces so they are flat.
- Arrange a teaspoon or so of each of the colourful chopped-up fruit in lines in the bowls, followed by the nuts and seeds, and finally tip the chia seeds into the last remaining space. Interesting to look at and interesting to eat ... colour-by-colour or mixed up to a smash.

Shred up your seeds and nuts to a baby-safe grainy/powdery texture with a sharp knife.

Baby shakshuka

Originally a North African recipe, over the generations shakshuka has become one of the signature dishes of *the* Middle East. The word means 'mixed up' and there are loads of variations, but this is a great weaning-friendly version. We have it for breakfast, but you can make it quickly any time of day. It's full of protein, fibre, fats, vitamins and minerals and, best of all, flavour. This makes an excellent sharing meal, just scatter the grown-ups' dishes with sliced fresh chilli and a pinch of salt.

FOR 2 ADULTS + 1 LITTLE ONE

WHAT DO I NEED?

1 onion, finely diced
1 pepper, finely diced
splash of olive oil
2 garlic clove
1 × 400ml can of plum tomatoes
¼ tsp ground cumin
3 eggs
large handful of coriander leaves, finely chopped

WHAT DO I DO?

- In your pan, soften the onion and pepper in a glug of olive oil. Cook for 4–5 mins over a medium heat, stirring often.
- When the vegetables are softened but not yet brown, squish/grate in the garlic and cook for a further minute. Add the tomatoes with some of the can's juice and the cumin. Stir to combine, bashing up the tomatoes with your spoon as you warm the mixture through. When things are looking well combined and sauce-like, create a dent in the sauce with the back of your spoon and crack the eggs in. Leave the pan on a very low heat for 4–5 mins (without stirring) while the eggs poach in the sauce.
- When the eggs are thoroughly cooked (the yolk should be set, not liquid), use a large spoon to carefully lift or slide the eggs and sauce into your bowls. Scatter with coriander and allow the little ones food to cool to a safe temperature. Depending on the teeth situ, serve the shakshuka straight-up or fork-mash together.

Pudding ... for breakfast

Chia is the king of seeds. This heavenly tasting dairy-, gluten – and refined-sugar-free little breakfast is nutrient dense and requires no cooking at all. Flavourless and easily digested, chia seeds boast an impressive list of vitamins and minerals, as well as fibre and high-quality plant-based protein. They absorb any liquid (and flavour), but this version is pretty special, bringing together a nutritional dream team: the mighty coconut; sweet, enzyme-packed mango and aromatic cinnamon, revered in various food cultures for its health-giving powers. This is a bit of a plan-ahead dish, but it'll keep in the fridge for three days and travels well – stash a pot under the pram.

FOR 2 ADULTS + 2 LITTLE ONES

WHAT DO I NEED?

3 tbsp chia seeds (any variety – I use black)
6 tbsp well-mashed soft, ripe mango
15 tbsp canned coconut milk (taken from a 400ml can)
½ tsp ground cinnamon

Topping

mashed banana, chopped blueberries and chopped nectarine

WHAT DO I DO?

- Put all the pudding ingredients into a couple of old jam jars or any other small lidded containers.
- Stir, put on the lids and pop it in the fridge. Leave for 2–3 hours or overnight, if possible.
- Spoon out into your bowls and serve with a quick fruit topping.

Banana bread PJ pancake stack

Healthy baby pancakes. Really? Aren't fried, fluffy pancakes a blow-out for special occasions? No! When your batter's this nutritious you can whip up a stack anytime you like. Pancakes make great finger food for your baby to explore. Unsatisfied with including just one banana bread recipe (see p.150), I wanted a way of bringing it to the breakfast table, too. Heart, prepare to sing.

FOR 2 ADULTS + 2 LITTLE ONES

WHAT DO I NEED?

2 tbsp coconut oil
2 eggs
1 banana, mashed very smoothly
6 tbsp flour (I use buckwheat or spelt)
1 tsp ground cinnamon
6 tbsp milk or water

Your choice of toppings

mashed banana
smooth nut butter
chia seeds
plain yoghurt

WHAT DO I DO?

- Heat 1 tbsp coconut oil in a frying pan while you mix your batter. Crack the eggs into a small mixing bowl. Add the banana, flour, cinnamon and milk or water. Whisk with a fork – you're looking for a 'thick soup' consistency. Tweak the flour and milk if needed.
- Pour several 6–8cm circles of batter into the pan to create mini pancakes. Don't overcrowd your pan. You'll know it's time to flip when the upper surface is no longer wet. Each pancake needs a minute on each side, max. Repeat with the remaining batter.
- Allow the pancakes to cool slightly before cutting into strips. Serve with a little more mashed banana, a drizzle of nut butter, a sprinkle of chia seeds and yoghurt for dunking.

A tablespoon of chia seeds soaked for 10 minutes in 2 tablespoons of water forms a gel that you can substitute for an egg in pancakes and baking. Great if your baby has any issues tolerating eggs, or if you're a vegan family.

Tropical dream PJ pancakes

If you're currently in the throes of teething, or one of those dreaded sleep regressions, this recipe will restore everybody's energy levels. The flour I use here brings slow-release carbohydrate; the egg packs in protein and all the big-hitting micronutrients; and the coconut milk is just a dream for little babies. So nutritious, so easily digested and so moreish. This recipe uses mashed mango, but you can sub that for banana if you like.

FOR 2 ADULTS + 2 LITTLE ONES

WHAT DO I NEED?

2 ripe mango 'cheeks' (yes that is indeed the culinary term … 1 fruit, minus the stone)
2 eggs
8 tsp flour (I use buckwheat or spelt)
1 × 400ml can coconut milk
2 tbsp coconut oil

Your choice of toppings

mashed banana
lime zest

WHAT DO I DO?

- Mash the mango until smooth with a fork and stir in the eggs, flour and coconut milk. Stir to combine, adding a little more flour or milk if needed to create a 'thick soup' texture.
- Heat a blob of coconut oil in your frying pan and drop in the batter to create 6–8cm circles. Allow them to cook for 1 minute, until the top no longer looks wet. Flip and cook for 30–60 seconds before removing the pancakes. Repeat with the remaining batter.
- Allow the pancakes to cool slightly before slicing, stacking and serving.
- Mash a couple of inches of banana to create a dunking dip, and add lime zest over the top if you'd like to add a zingy, bitter flavour for the baby to explore.

You can bury treasure in the pancakes by pressing pieces of blueberry, strawberry or raspberry into the wet top surface while the batter is cooking. Allow to cook for about a minute, then flip carefully, ensuring the berries remain embedded, and cook for a further minute or so. When both sides are golden, and the berries are slightly brown and caramelised, remove from the pan and allow to cool slightly before serving.

Often out and about
and on the move,
I need lunch food
that's easily portable.

On-the-go lunches, snacks + side orders

For busy parents of busy babies, lunch often happens on the fly around naptimes, playdates and errands. The meals and snacks in this chapter work just as well out and about as at home in the highchair – they travel well and aren't (horrendously) messy.

As well as quick little lunches, many of these recipes do double duty as nutritious 'side orders' to add to some of the dinner recipes you'll see later in the book.

Sweet potato toast with PB + J

This really is a magic little meal. Inspired by one of the biggest Instagram food trends, sweet potato toast has to be seen to be believed. This is my twist on the American childhood classic, peanut butter and jelly, which my brother and I got heavily into the summer our parents took us to Disneyworld when we were little.

FOR 2 ADULTS + 2 LITTLE ONES

WHAT DO I NEED?

2 sweet potatoes, skin on
smooth nut butter
6 fresh raspberries
¼ tsp ground cinnamon

WHAT DO I DO?

- Using a carving knife, carefully slice the raw sweet potatoes lengthways to create 1cm slices that resemble the shape of a slice of bread.
- Put two slices into your toaster and start toasting. Keep an eye on your pieces as they cook – they should need about 3 minutes of cooking time, although it will of course vary a bit. Remove your slices and check they're cooked through. You're looking for a soft, marshmallowy texture in the centre of the slice with crispy edges. Repeat with the other slices.
- Spread your nut butter on top, then scatter with pieces of fresh raspberry and a quick dusting of cinnamon. Cut into grippable pieces for your baby.
- Why not add lashings of Superbaby superjam too? Find it on p.152.

Corn fritters

Here we're combining fibre-rich corn and protein-rich eggs to create soft little hand-held fritters that you can serve warm or cold, solo or with some dips and toppings. They take moments to make and are fun to eat.

FOR 1 ADULT + 1 LITTLE ONE

WHAT DO I NEED?

2 eggs
6 tbsp flour (I use spelt or buckwheat)
splash of milk, or your baby's usual milk
¼ tsp paprika
1 × 198g can of sweetcorn, drained
olive oil

Toppings

2 tsp plain yoghurt
grated Cheddar

WHAT DO I DO?

- Crack the eggs into a mixing bowl and add the flour, milk and paprika. Whisk to combine.
- Tip the corn into a different bowl and use a potato masher to rough up the kernels, breaking them apart a little. This is just a precaution to ensure the sweetcorn pieces don't pose a choking risk. Add the bashed-up corn to the batter and stir to combine.
- Splash olive oil into a flat frying pan and bring it to a medium heat. Using a spoon, drop in 5–7cm circles of batter, perhaps two or three at a time – it's easier if the pan isn't overcrowded. Cook for a minute or so before flipping. When both sides are golden and toasted, remove from the pan and leave to cool on a paper towel. Repeat until all the batter is gone (you should yield roughly twelve fritters).
- Serve the fritters with yoghurt and cheese. To create a more substantial lunch, combine with the Baby guac on p.72 or a mashed-up poached egg (allow the yolk to cook thoroughly).

Buildable baby mezze

The following recipes work brilliantly alone or combined to make a beautifully nutritious and well-balanced mezze meal that the whole family can share and enjoy.

Baby hummus

Hummus is always a crowd pleaser, but the shop-bought stuff can contain a fair bit of added salt. By combining chickpeas with tahini we bring together all nine amino acids needed by the body. If you're concerned about a possible sesame allergy, leave out the tahini. If your baby has reflux or eczema, you can easily omit the lemon juice … its citric acid is thought to aggravate those conditions in some babies.

The traffic light game
Make traffic light hummus by dividing this yield into three. One third stays plain (yellow), whizz a slice of cooked beetroot or a fresh cherry tomato into one third (red), and two small raw spinach leaves into the next (green). Blob of each on a plate and grab a toy car. Beep beep.

FOR 2 ADULTS + 2 LITTLE ONES

WHAT DO I NEED?
1 × 400g can chickpeas, rinsed
1 garlic clove, squished or grated
2 tbsp tahini
4 tbsp olive oil
4 tbsp lemon juice
4 tbsp cold water

WHAT DO I DO?
Tumble everything into a blender and pulse to a thick, smooth, creamy consistency. You may need to stop and stir the mixture a couple of times to ensure it blends evenly. If it's a bit too thick, add an extra splash of cold water.

To serve, try making edible spoons by roasting wedges of butternut squash or sweet potato (high in vitamin A, fibre and slow-release carbs) for 30 mins at 200°C/fan 180°C/Gas mark 6 with a bit of olive oil, shaking the tray occasionally. If you're in a hurry, just serve with cucumber sticks or fingers of wholemeal toast.

Baba-ganoush (and mama-ganoush)

Aubergine. Not an obvious choice for baby food, but it's easy to find, pretty good value and ever so nutritious. Full of fibre and B-vits, it contains rare-ish minerals like copper (iron transport) and manganese (energy metabolism and healthy bones). However, it's garlic and parsley that are the stars of the show here. More than just flavourings, they're nutrient-laden wonder foods in their own right. Add lots of lemon juice and sea salt to yours. This is great on top of a jacket sweet potato.

FOR 2 ADULTS + 2 LITTLE ONES

WHAT DO I NEED?

1 whole aubergine
½ garlic clove, squashed or grated
small handful of parsley leaves
zest and juice of ¼ lemon

WHAT DO I DO?

• Bake the aubergine on a baking tray at 200°C/fan 180°C/Gas mark 6 for 40 mins, having poked it a few times with a knife. It will soften, shrink slightly and the skin will blacken.
• Remove from the oven and let cool before slicing and scooping the flesh into a blender (discard the skin). Add the garlic, parsley and lemon zest and juice. Pulse until smooth and serve with oatcake crackers (see p.87).

Baby falafels

Falafels are hugely popular right across the Middle East and comes in countless regional variations. I first tried them in Israel when I was nine, and nowadays anytime I'm in Paris I'll head to the Marais district for a street-stall falafel wrap. Chickpeas form the basis of this dish. Cheap and easy to stash in the cupboard, they're packed with protein. I've added oats to boost the fibre and mineral load of this dish, but kept it traditional with the herbs and spices.

FOR 2 ADULTS + 2 LITTLE ONES

WHAT DO I NEED?

1 x 400g can chickpeas, rinsed
4 tsp oats
1 large garlic clove
1 tsp ground cumin
handful of parsley stalks and leaves
olive oil

Toppings

plain yoghurt
grated cucumber

WHAT DO I DO?

• Tip the rinsed chickpeas onto paper towels or a clean tea towel and pat them dry. Pour them into your blender with all the other ingredients and whizz to a thick paste.
• Warm a couple of tablespoons of olive oil in a pan. Spoon in small balls of the falafel mixture, turning and flipping them as they gently cook for 3–4 minutes over a medium heat. You will need to cook these in batches. Turn out onto paper towels, allow to cool, then serve with a blob of yoghurt and some grated cucumber.

Baby guac with crunchy cucumber nachos

When new teeth attack, Baby B's appetite is low. One day I sat her on the counter and she watched me make this colourful smash-up. A little bowlful, served gum-numbingly cold, perked her right up. Avocado is an incredible first food, thought of as one of nature's 'perfect' foods because it contains pretty much everything we need to survive. It's been linked with improved wound healing and reduction of inflammation – useful for a sore-gummed babe – and contains vitamins A, B1, B2, B6, C, E, K; minerals potassium, phosphorus, calcium and iron; and trace amounts of selenium, copper and zinc.

FOR 2 ADULTS + 2 LITTLE ONES

WHAT DO I NEED?

1 soft, ripe avocado
4 cherry tomatoes
½ small garlic clove
1 tsp lime juice
cucumber sticks, cooled in the fridge, to serve

WHAT DO I DO?

- Couldn't be easier. Put everything in a blender and whizz until completely smooth, or pulse for a chunkier texture. Add a splash of iced water if it's looking a bit too thick (avocados vary in texture as they ripen). Tip into a couple of bowls and let your baby play, dunking in the cold cucumber sticks.
- If you have any leftovers, you could add this to the Baby burrito bowl (see p.100), Brazilian baby jackets (see p.114) or Huevos rancheros (see p.49).

Instead of salty, hard nachos, cucumber sticks are easy to hold (leave skin on for grip) and full of water for hydration. Perfect for angry gums.

Buildable baby frittatas

Frittatas (baked omelettes) are my favourite way to introduce a baby to the wonder of egg. All sorts of ingredients work, while the cheese brings flavour, texture and a lovely golden colour, as well as some extra protein and calcium.

MAKES 6 BIG OR 12 MINI ONES

WHAT DO I NEED?

1 egg
splash of your baby's usual milk
pinch of dried herbs or a couple of leaves of fresh parsley/coriander/basil
1 tbsp grated Cheddar

Your choice of additions

leftovers like cold salmon or shredded cooked meat
steamed broccoli
sweet potato mash
squashed peas or chickpeas
canned tuna
torn-up spinach
grated courgette
peas and ham
diced tomato or avocado

WHAT DO I DO?

- Preheat the oven to 200°C/fan 180°C/Gas mark 6. Fork-whisk the egg in a jug/bowl with a splash of milk. Add your herbs, stir, then divide the mixture across a 12-hole mini muffin tin or a 6-hole regular-size muffin tray (non-stick ideally, or grease with olive oil). Fill each hole only halfway to leave space for your additions.
- Submerge small pieces of anything you're using into the egg mixture, then scatter a fat pinch of cheese across the top of every frittata. Bake for 10 minutes (check they're set by putting a knife in and checking it comes out clean and not covered in wet mixture).
- Allow the whole tray to cool before turning out and serving. Spares will keep in an airtight container in the fridge for 3 days. Perfect as a hand-held snack or split and spread with mashed avocado.

An egg is just about the most efficient and best value food on the planet. Complete protein, well-balanced fats and essential minerals and vitamins in combinations you don't find anywhere else. The WHO advises that well-cooked eggs are safe from 6 months. Egg allergies are not common, but if your baby vomits after eating egg, speak to the doctor. It's often egg whites that babies disagree with, so you can introduce them by using only the yolk (where the bulk of micronutrients are found). This can be made with two yolks instead of one whole egg.

Dunkin' doughnuts

Now, these aren't technically doughnuts. But with all kinds of interactive sticky dips and sprinkles, they're just as fun. Promise. And so quick.

FOR 1 LITTLE ONE

WHAT DO I NEED?
1 apple, skin on

Your choice of sticky toppings
smooth nut butter
mashed banana
Superbaby superjam (see p.152)
plain thick Greek yoghurt

Your choice of baby-safe sprinkles
chia seeds
chopped fresh blueberries, strawberries, raspberries
diced kiwi, mango or peach
ground almonds or ground sunflower or pumpkin seeds
sweet spices like ground nutmeg, cinnamon or cardamom

WHAT DO I DO?
• Wash and core your apple, then carefully slice it into thin discs. Spread with your sticky topping, then scatter with your chosen sprinkles.
• A perfect quick and nourishing little treat that's super interesting to explore

The easiest ever baking recipes – you don't even need to bother with weighing scales.

Breads, crackers + savoury bakes

Cooking's pretty creative and flexible, but baking's precise … a formula. Can we bake without faffing around with weighing scales? Can we make bread without complicated methods involving yeast and dough proving? Can we make light, fluffy, tasty things without refined white flour? Baby B and I spent many afternoons experimenting in our kitchen. The verdict? YES. Yes we can.

I'll come onto sweet bakes later on in the book, but for now, here are my hero savoury bakes, including a genius little recipe for homemade teething biscuits. Preheat that oven.

Homemade teething biscuits

I was quite shocked reading the ingredients lists of some of the commercially manufactured teething biscuits. Lots are just a blend of refined flours, cheap fats, refined sugar and chemical vitamin fortification. My alternative is a simple two-ingredient biscuit, one of the all-time most popular recipes on my blog. The biscuits are firm enough to stand up to serious gumming and chewing without disintegrating into a mess of gooey crumbs, but not so tough that they'll damage tender gums. There is of course naturally occurring fruit sugar in the banana – it's still sugar, but it brings with it micronutrients – and fibre that slows the fruit sugar's release into the baby's bloodstream.

MAKES 10–15 BISCUITS

WHAT DO I NEED?

1 banana
1 teacup of porridge oats (whizzed into flour in your blender)

Your choice of additions

½ tsp ground ginger or finely grated fresh ginger
OR
finely grated zest of ¼ lemon

WHAT DO I DO?

- Preheat the oven to 200°C/fan 180°C/Gas mark 6. Mash the banana very smoothly and mix with the oats using a fork, adding either flavour addition now if you're including one. It will feel like you need more liquid in this dough, but stay strong. Keep mixing. A firm dough will come together just as you're losing hope.
- Use wet hands to form any shapes your baby will like. I make sticks and fist-sized discs. It will yield 10 to 15 biscuits from this amount of mixture. Arrange them on a non-stick baking tray and bake for 12–15 mins until pale golden. The biscuits will feel firm and crunchy, and will become crispier still as they cool.
- Once completely cold, store in an airtight jar. They'll keep for 5–7 days and travel brilliantly … don't leave home without them!

BB bread

This recipe was my holy grail, the one I researched most and tested more than any other: easy, tasty homemade bread with no refined grains and no complicated multiple-step process of kneading and proving. I can't claim all the credit for this recipe – it was the result of plenty of chats with our local baker who tasted lots of my attempts. This yeast-free recipe won out as our favourite. It's soft and easy to eat, toasts nicely, and is easy to make … even with a baby on your hip. It's rather an expensive recipe, but freezes well and with the quantities a baby eats, a batch goes a long way.

MAKES 1 LOAF OR 6 ROLLS

WHAT DO I NEED?

2 eggs, lightly beaten
¾ teacup of ground flax/linseed (about 75g)
¼ teacup of ground almonds (about 25g)
2 tbsp lemon juice
3–4 tbsp cold water
½ tsp bicarbonate soda
1½ tbsp coconut oil, melted

WHAT DO I DO?

- Preheat the oven to 200°C/fan 180°C/Gas mark 6. Combine everything in a mixing bowl and stir well until a stiff batter forms. Leave for 5 minutes to help thicken. If you'd like to make a loaf, pour it into a well-greased 450g loaf tin. If you'd like to make a batch of rolls, grease a baking tray and spoon 2 tablespoons of the mixture per bun, forming six rolls. Smooth the tops with slightly wet hands.
- Bake for 20 minutes (loaf) or 15 minutes (rolls). You'll know the bake is done when the bread's surface is golden and a metal knife comes out clean, rather than coated in wet batter.
- Leave the bread to cool on a wire rack (the metal rack from your oven's grill makes a great cooling station). The bread will become crisp and firm as it cools. The bread will keep for three days in an airtight box in the fridge and is safe to reheat.

Stovetop flatbreads

Another super-quick, super-simple bread recipe. These soft, tear-able flatbreads are lovely served warm with smashed avocado, falafel (see p.70) or cream cheese, or as a dipping accompaniment to the curries, chillies, tagines and stews you'll find in the Dinnertime section (see p.90). You can add finely chopped fresh herbs or a pinch or two of an aromatic spice like cumin or paprika, if you like.

MAKES 8 FLATBREADS

WHAT DO I NEED?

2 teacups of spelt/wholewheat flour (around 200g)
2 tbsp plain yoghurt
2 tbsp olive oil
2 tsp baking powder
8 tbsp warm water

WHAT DO I DO?

- Put all the ingredients into a mixing bowl and, using clean hands (or just one if you're #OneHandCooking), knead the mix for a couple of minutes until a dough forms. Leave the dough to rest for 10 minutes, placing a tea towel over the bowl.
- Divide the mixture into eight and scatter some flour onto your countertop. Using a floured rolling pin (or if you're me, a clean wine bottle), roll out discs around 15cm in diameter.
- While you're rolling the first disc, warm a large, flat pan to a medium heat. Lay the disc very carefully into the pan (no oil), then cover with a lid and allow the bread to cook for 90 seconds. Remove the lid, flip and let the bread cook for a further 90 seconds on the other side. Repeat with remaining discs. Voila. Soft, fresh, homemade flatbreads.

Oatcake crackers

Once B popped a few teeth and started enjoying crispy, crunchy textures, I was on the look out for crackers that weren't salty or artificially flavoured. One day I tried making my own and have been using this recipe ever since. They're crisp and crunchy, but won't shatter into shards that could hurt little gums. I pack them up for pram expeditions, pre-built into little snacks: a slice of banana stuck down with nut butter; a few slices of cheese or a pot of hummus to dip.

MAKES 14–16 CRACKERS

WHAT DO I NEED?

1 teacup of porridge oats (whizzed into flour in your blender)
4 tbsp olive oil or melted butter

Your choice of additions

2 tsp finely grated cheese
pinch of any dried herb
twist of black pepper

WHAT DO I DO?

- Preheat the oven to 200°C/fan 180°C/Gas mark 6 and grease a baking sheet with butter or olive oil. Tip the oats into a bowl and add the oil/melted butter. Add any extras now. Stir with a wooden spoon or knead with your hands. Once a soft ball of dough has formed, turn it out onto a floured surface.
- Grab a clean, dry bottle of wine to use as a rolling pin (or use a rolling pin if you must!). Roll your dough out until it's about 2mm thick, about the thickness of a coin. You might need to scatter a little extra flour as you roll to prevent the dough from sticking.
- Take a small drinking glass/espresso cup and press out discs of dough, placing them onto the baking sheet. Repeat cutting and rolling until you've used all your dough and filled your baking sheet. You should have 14 to 16 crackers. If you've added cheese to your dough, grate a little extra over the surface to add a golden crunch on top.
- Bake for 20 minutes or until firm, crisp and ever-so-slightly golden. Allow to cool, then store in an airtight container for up to a week. If they go a little soft, crisp them back up by placing in a warm oven for a minute or two.

Courgette + cheese muffins

These were the first things I ever baked for Baby B, when she was about 8 months old and very interested in picking up and holding her food. I wanted to create a tasty, soft and well-balanced savoury muffin that could act as a hand-held snack by itself, or become part of a more substantial meal. This recipe brings together slow-release carbohydrate and protein, as well as fibre from the courgette, which, along with the cheese, keeps this muffin nice and moist.

MAKES 6 BIG OR 12 MINI

WHAT DO I NEED?

6 tbsp spelt flour
½ tsp baking powder
pinch of dried rosemary
½ courgette, grated
3 tbsp grated Cheddar
1 egg, beaten
3 tbsp whole cow's milk (or your baby's usual milk)
2 tbsps olive oil or melted butter

WHAT DO I DO?

• Preheat the oven to 200°C/fan 180°C/Gas mark 6. Put the dry ingredients into a mixing bowl and add the wet ingredients, stirring well to bring together a stiff batter. If you're #OneHandCooking, rest your mixing bowl on a folded tea towel to keep it still while you mix.

• Divide the mixture across a muffin tray – this will make around 6 regular ones or 12 mini-sized muffins. Bake for 10–15 minutes until the muffins appear golden. Plunge a knife into a muffin and if it comes out clean, they're cooked.

• Turn the muffins out and allow to cool slightly before serving. These are lovely served fresh from the oven – break one open and you'll see the melted cheese throughout – or split and spread with mashed avocado. They're also great as a dunkable accompaniment to any stew, soup or curry-type dish.

• Spares will keep in an airtight container for three days and are safe to reheat before serving.

Every recipe in this
chapter will create
social sharing dinners
where your baby's
the star of the show.

Dinnertime

Dinnertime. The end of a good day's babying, and a parent's chance to fuel everyone up for the long, uninterrupted night's sleep ahead (LOL). Stress has no place at our dinner table, so I've devised these recipes to help you put something tasty, nutritious and interesting on the table in minutes.

These dinners are so tasty you'll want to eat them yourself. And you can. One meal, one family. So not only are we bringing our babies to the family table, but what *they're* having is so nice, it's inspiring what *we're* having? How great is that?

Tuna niçoise smash

Way before B was on the scene, B's dad and I went on a surf trip to Portugal. Maybe I should have been concentrating a bit harder on the surfing, but the thing that sticks in my mind is the canned tuna. Next level flavoursome, unctuous and zingy, we couldn't get enough of it. When it came to working fish into B's diet, I just had to find a way for her to experience that sunny niçoise vibe. Tuna is protein-rich and packed with omega 3 fatty acids, such as docosahexaenoic acid (DHA) that helps with brain function and vision. Avocado brings vitamins A>K and all the big-hitting minerals. Hard-boiled eggs take this dish up a notch, and cucumber sticks bring some dunkable fun as well as vitamin C and dietary fibre.

FOR 1 ADULT + 2 LITTLE ONES

WHAT DO I NEED?

8 new potatoes
3 eggs
160g can tuna (canned in olive oil, unsalted)
2 ripe avocados
cucumber sticks, for dunking
a large handful of lettuce leaves
olive oil
splash of vinegar

WHAT DO I DO?

- Boil the new potatoes and eggs in a large pan (or in two separate pans) for 10 minutes until the eggs are hard-boiled and the potatoes are soft.
- While they're cooling, roughly mash half a can of fish with the avocado. De-shell the eggs under running water and roughly fork-mash two of the eggs into half the soft potato. Combine the tuna-avo mix with the egg-potato mix, spoon your babies portion into a bowl and mash together to a consistency your baby will like.
- Serve via a combination of cucumber dunkers and a baby spoon.
- For the grown-up, top lettuce leaves with unmashed tuna, sliced egg and sliced potato. Drizzle over olive oil, a splash of vinegar and some black pepper.

Nutritionally, canned fish is not the poor relation of fresh fish. Of course fresh food always has the nutritional edge, but tuna is preserved in a timeless, natural and chemical-free way: sealed in a can, the fish can't spoil and retains much of its nutrient load.

Buckwheat risotto

Sadly, the traditional arborio rice in risotto doesn't bring a whole lot to the party, nutritionally. Buckwheat is a very easy switch. My B eats so little (and throws/drops so much ...) that any food surviving the voyage from bowl to mouth needs to bring as much goodness as possible. With eight of the nine essential amino acids, we're taking care of the baby's protein requirements without having to reach for meat/fish/egg. High on B-vits, buckwheat also delivers iron, zinc, phosphorus and magnesium. Mushrooms bring an interesting savoury flavour that's unusual for a baby, plus selenium and vitamin C. Cheddar adds calcium and fat.

FOR 2 ADULTS + 2 LITTLE ONES

WHAT DO I NEED?

2 small onions, diced
olive oil
4 garlic cloves, squished or grated
8 white mushrooms, diced
8 tbsp whole buckwheat (about 120g)
4 mugfuls of Baby-friendly bone broth (see p.119) (about 1 litre)
grated Cheddar, to serve

WHAT DO I DO?

- Soften the diced onion in a warm pan that's been splashed with olive oil. Add the squished garlic and mushrooms, stirring for 3–4 minutes until the vegetables soften. Tip in the rinsed buckwheat and stir to coat. Add quarter of the liquid gradually, stirring to absorb. This will take maybe 15–20 mins, but it's real one-hand-cooking ... the baby can watch from your hip.
- When it's creamy and soft, taste to check it's nicely cooked, then sprinkle in the cheese and stir to melt.

No-roast chicken pot roast

This tastes like one of those velvety, oozy casseroles that's been lazing away in the oven all afternoon while you read the papers. Except I make it in about 20 minutes with a flappy-arm hooting munchkin waving a carrot at me. The rich flavour comes from twice-cooking the chicken. First it browns and sizzles, then softly poaches. The thigh is a cheap cut that has loads of flavour, and leaving the meat on the bone for the cooking process gives this dish bone-broth vibes. The vegetables bring plenty of fibre and minerals, notably beta carotene in the carrot and iron, calcium and folate in the green leafies. And because the vegetables aren't cooked for hours on end, they retain more nutritional value.

FOR 2 ADULTS + 2 LITTLE ONES

WHAT DO I NEED?

splash of olive oil
6 chicken thighs, skin on
2 small onions or 1 leek, diced
2 small garlic cloves, squished or grated
2 tsp mixed herbs
2 carrots, diced
6 small potatoes, diced
a couple of large handfuls of spinach or cabbage greens, sliced
6 mugfuls of cold water, Baby-friendly bone broth (see p.119) or salt-free bouillon/stock (about 1½ litres)

WHAT DO I DO?

- Heat a glug of olive oil in a large pan. When it's hot, place the chicken in the pan and sear on all sides, which will take a minute or two. You're not cooking it through, just browning the exterior.
- When it's golden all over, add your onion or leek, garlic and herbs, and allow them to heat through for a minute before pouring in the stock/broth/water. Throw in the diced carrot and potato and put a lid on. Simmer for 15–20 minutes, adding the sliced greens for the final couple of minutes.
- Check the chicken is cooked through, then remove the pan from the heat. For your little ones portions, lift out the chicken and use a knife and fork to shred the meat away from the skin and bone. Add to a bowl with some of the veg mixture and leave everything to cool slightly before serving up or transferring to your blender to whizz to your baby's preferred texture. You can always leave a few pieces intact to serve as finger food, making this meal fun and interactive. Any leftovers will freeze well for another time.

Baby bouillabaisse

Bouillabaisse was originally the staple dish of fishermen in the Mediterranean port city of Marseille, a city we passed through *en famille* last year. Bouillabaisse means 'boil and reduce', but this quick baby-friendly version can be made quickly. White fish is a lovely food to build a weaning meal around: soft and easy to eat, it's full of nutrients. Fennel is a really unusual addition to a baby dish but it's such a beautiful and complex flavour to introduce, plus it's packed with dietary fibre, potassium, folate and vitamin C. We found herbes de Provence in a market near Marseille and brought them home to make this. It's a mix of rosemary, thyme and oregano that's traditional to the region.

FOR 2 ADULTS + 2 LITTLE ONES

WHAT DO I NEED?

splash of olive oil
2 small onions, finely diced
1 bulb of fennel, finely diced
3 garlic cloves, squished or grated
½ tsp herbes de Provence (or pinches of dried oregano, rosemary and thyme)
24 cherry tomatoes, quartered (about 250g)
8 new potatoes, diced
4 mugfuls of cold water (about 1 litre)
2 fillets of any white fish, skinned and deboned

WHAT DO I DO?

- Put a splash of olive oil in a saucepan and heat until the oil is hot. Add the onion and fennel, stirring for 5 minutes until they go a little soft and translucent. Add the garlic, dried herbs and cherry tomatoes and stir-cook-stir for a further 5 minutes. Now add the potatoes and the water. Pop the lid on and bring to a simmer for 10 minutes.
- Remove the lid and add the fish, stirring to coat them in the stew mix. Put the lid on and allow the fish to cook for 4 minutes – it'll flake and break apart when thoroughly cooked. Remove the pan from the heat and allow to cool slightly before serving.
- A quick fork-mash (or a whizz in the blender) for your little one and it's *bon appétit*.

Gentle lentil dhal

Red lentils. The king of baby foods? Quite possibly. Protein. Fibre. Iron. B-vits. Vit-C. Beta carotene (a compound that the body converts into vit-A). Dhal is quick to cook, great value and has a creamy texture perfect for anyone low on teeth/sore of gum. This recipe is inspired by the unreal thali café that pops up at the market near our house every Saturday (along with a half-mile-long queue of hungry fans).

FOR 2 ADULTS + 2 LITTLE ONES

WHAT DO I NEED?

2 tbsp olive or coconut oil
2 small red onions, diced
3 garlic cloves, squished or grated
2 tsp peeled fresh ginger, grated
2 tsp ground turmeric
2 tsp ground cumin
8 tbsp red lentils
½ a 400ml can of coconut milk
12 tbsp cold water, Baby-friendly bone broth (see p.119) or salt-free bouillon/stock (about 180ml)
1 tbsp plain yoghurt, to serve

WHAT DO I DO?

- Heat up a pan, adding a couple of tsps of olive or coconut oil. Throw in the onion and stir. Once the onion is starting to soften and become translucent, add the garlic and ginger. Heat and stir for 1 minute before adding the dry spices, lentils, coconut milk and water/broth/stock and bringing to a gentle simmer. Stir, lady. It's like making porridge. Keep everything moving.
- After 10–12 minutes things will be looking very creamy and smelling very tasty. Taste to check everything's well cooked, then transfer a couple of tablespoons to your baby's bowl and allow to cool slightly before serving, with a little blob of plain yoghurt on top if you like. You made dhal! With one hand!

Baby burrito bowl

I became very attached to our local Mexican restaurant while I was pregnant. Always a burrito, always super spicy. There's loads of scientific evidence that unborn babies can detect the flavours in their mothers' food via the amniotic fluid ... perhaps that's why Baby B is crazy for this dish. Or maybe it's because there's so much interesting stuff going on: textures, colours and tastes. Sweet potato, avocado and black beans would be a well-balanced feast by themselves, but here we're adding beef and dairy to the fiesta as well.

FOR 2 ADULTS + 2 LITTLE ONES

WHAT DO I NEED?

splash of olive oil
10 tbsp minced beef (about 150g)
2 small garlic cloves, squished or grated
10 tbsp canned black beans (about 150g)
½ tsp paprika
½ tsp ground cumin
1 heaped tbsp tomato purée
2 small sweet potatoes, peeled and grated
2 mugfuls of cold water, Baby-friendly bone broth (see p.119) or salt-free bouillon/stock

To serve

Baby guac (see p.72)
1 tbsp plain yoghurt
pinch of grated cheese
squeeze of lime juice
brown rice

WHAT DO I DO?

- Warm a glug of olive oil in a small pan and add the beef mince and garlic. Stir it around for a couple of minutes to ensure the meat becomes brown all over. Add the black beans, paprika, cumin, tomato purée and sweet potato. Pour in the water/broth/stock and bring to a gentle simmer for 14–16 mins, mushing up the beans a bit with your stirring spoon.
- While your chilli is cooking, mix up a batch of Baby guac or just fork-mash a quarter avocado.
- When the chilli is cooked, heap some into bowls and allow to cool slightly before topping each with your guac/smashed avo, a teaspoon of plain yoghurt and some grated cheese. Squeeze of lime, party time.
- If you're serving this with rice, you can have it boiling away while you're preparing the chilli, so everything's ready at once.

Add chilli and salt to the adults portions if you want more of a kick. This freezes beautifully if you fancy a bit of batch-cooking.

Sardine ragu

This 7-minute dinner mostly comes out of a can, but it's crazy nutritious and a great way to get some important omega 3 fatty acids into your baby. Sardines contain complete protein, calcium, iron, potassium and almost no risk of heavy metal contaminants (such as mercury). Plus an unusual piquant flavour for those courageous little taste buds. The vegetables bring fibre and vitamin C, plus lycopene in the tomatoes and blood-strengthening iron in the dark green leafies. I've got cavolo nero (aka dinosaur kale) here, but spinach, curly kale or dark cabbage-y greens are also great. I'm using spelt pasta because it's high in good-quality carbs and contains heaps more protein than regular white pasta.

FOR 2 ADULTS + 2 LITTLE ONES

WHAT DO I NEED?

1 red onion, finely diced
4 garlic cloves, squished or grated
splash of oil
2 courgettes, grated
a couple of large handful of greens/kale/spinach, finely sliced
2 × 120g can sardine fillets, any skin and bones removed
½ tsp dried oregano
1 × 400g can plum tomatoes

To serve

200g spelt spaghetti strands, snapped in half
handful of grated cheese

WHAT DO I DO?

- Sweat the onion and garlic in the olive oil for 2 minutes on a medium heat. Add the courgettes, sliced greens, sardines, oregano and tomatoes, plus a couple of splashes of the can's juice. Stir and sweat for 5–6 mins.
- Meanwhile, cook the spaghetti according to the packet instructions. When cooked, drain and mix with the sauce.
- Depending where you are with motor skills and teeth, serve it as it comes, or chop it up with a knife and fork to make this dinner spoonable. Put cheese on top if you like.

Sardines don't scream 'baby food', but there are few finer and more efficient ingredients you could serve.

Magic fish fingers + crushy peas

A traditional British fish supper is one of the finest things in life. This recipe came about on holiday in Cornwall last summer with Baby B's grandparents, aunt, uncle and cousins. Freshly landed fish and traditional mushy peas, baby style. But instead of those radioactive-green chip-shop processed peas ... meet crushy peas: lightly cooked so their protein – and vitamin-load remains much more intact, they taste great and take seconds (you can also make them minty if you like). The cheap and cheerful pea is underrated. They have more vitamin C than apples and more fibre than wholemeal bread. Yes, peas.

FOR 2 ADULTS + 2 LITTLE ONES

WHAT DO I NEED?

2 fillets of any boneless white fish, skinned and sliced into 1cm mini fingers
3 eggs, beaten
12–16 tbsp ground almonds (about 240g)
olive oil
4 generous handfuls of frozen peas
2 tsp butter
splash of milk or water
a few mint leaves, torn up (optional)

WHAT DO I DO?

- One-hand cooking at its finest. Dip your fish slices in beaten egg, then roll them in ground almonds.
- Fry the fish fingers in a little olive oil for 5 minutes, turning regularly (you may need to do this in batches), or bake in the oven at 200°C/fan 180°C/Gas mark 6 for 8–10 mins, turning once.
- While they're cooking, make your crushy peas. Steam the frozen peas for 3–4 minutes, then tumble them into your blender with the butter and a tiny splash of milk or water. Pulse for a few seconds to create a texture your baby will like: a bit chunky or completely smooth. Add a few torn-up mint leaves to the blender if you'd like to experiment with minted peas (I grew mine in the garden! First thing I've grown since infant school).
- Heap the peas onto your baby's plate next to a little stack of fish fingers. Serve with some boiled new potatoes or Rainbow root fries (see p. 130) if you like. Ahoy there, full tummy.

Baby green curry

Coconut, ginger, garlic and coriander are the pillars of Thai cooking and all four combine here into a rich, aromatic curry. You could easily use white fish or chicken, but the protein source in this version is chickpeas. Butternut squash adds depth and sweetness, and thickens the sauce into a creamy stew-like consistency that's more practical for a babe than the more typical thin/watery green curry sauce. I serve this with steamed brown rice.

FOR 2 ADULTS + 2 LITTLE ONES

WHAT DO I NEED?

Green curry paste

2–3cm peeled fresh ginger
1 garlic clove, peeled
½ red onion, roughly diced
hand-sized bunch of coriander (stalks and leaves)
1 tsp low/no-salt Thai fish sauce (a potent reduction of anchovies, rich in the rare-ish savoury flavour umami)
4 tbsp water

Curry

1 tsp coconut oil
1 butternut squash, diced
1 × 400g can chickpeas, rinsed
½ of a 400ml can coconut milk (200ml)
1 mugful of cold water + 1 tsp salt-free vegetable bouillon/stock or 1 mugful of Baby-friendly bone broth (see p.119)

WHAT DO I DO?

- Put all the green curry paste ingredients into a blender and whizz smooth.
- Warm the coconut oil in a medium-sized saucepan and pour the paste in. Heat gently for 2 minutes, then add the butternut squash and chickpeas. Stir to coat everything in curry paste, then add the coconut milk and stock/broth. Bring to a simmer and cook for 12–14 minutes, lid on.
- Next, the secret weapon: a potato masher. Softly mash the mixture to break down the squash and chickpeas, achieving a creamy-textured curry that you won't need to put through the blender for your baby. Serve family-style over rice. Grown-ups can top theirs with sliced fresh chilli, lime and soy sauce. Wear bibs ... everyone!

Melting middle meatballs

These stay super soft and juicy because of an important little twist: the binding ingredient here is ground almonds instead of the traditional breadcrumbs. As well as dietary fibre, vitamin E and some powerful essential minerals, the natural plant fats make these soft enough for a weaning baby to eat. Don't serve these up too hot ... we don't want molten cheese anywhere near the babies. Warm and squidgy is perfect. They also work served cold as a portable pram snack, and freeze well (uncooked) so are ideal for batch-cooking.

FOR 2 ADULTS + 2 LITTLE ONES

WHAT DO I NEED?

12 tbsp minced beef (about 180g)
8 tbsp ground almonds
1 tsp dried oregano
large handful of grated Cheddar
splash of olive oil

To serve (optional)

200g wholewheat/spelt spaghetti strands, snapped in half and cooked, with 3 tbsp canned chopped tomatoes stirred through (the heat of the cooked pasta will warm the tomatoes)

WHAT DO I DO?

- Put the minced beef in a bowl with the ground almonds and oregano. Mix with a fork, then with wet hands grab a small handful of the mix in one hand and use the other to press a fat pinch of grated Cheddar into the meat before rolling between your palms to create a ball, sealing the cheese inside. Repeat with the rest of the mixture.
- Warm a frying pan, add a splash of olive oil and place the balls in to cook for around 5 minutes – you may need to do this in batches. Swirl the pan regularly to encourage them to cook evenly. 5 minutes later, you will have beautiful, toasted meatballs. Check one to make sure the meat is cooked through, then allow to cool to a safe serving temperature.
- Great served straight up, or balanced on top of a little swirl of pasta. If you prefer to spoon-feed, don't be put off this recipe: they are easy to fork-mash and scoop. Try mashing a couple of balls with a quarter of ripe avocado to create a lovely, spoon-able dish.

Mini slider burgers

If you fancy a family burger night, create the same mixture, but mix the grated cheese throughout before forming mini patties that you can fry, bake or BBQ. Sandwich inside a BB bread roll (see p.80) with a side of Rainbow root fries (see p.130).

Baby biryani

Biryani is a simple, satisfying meal eaten daily in India, and it is packed with antioxidant - and mineral-rich cumin, cinnamon, turmeric, cloves, ginger and garlic. Perfect for an adventurous young weanling. I use brown rice as it's more nutritious than white.

FOR 2 ADULTS + 2 LITTLE ONES

WHAT DO I NEED?

8 tbsp olive oil
2 red onions, 1 finely diced and 1 finely sliced
2 tsp any flour
4 garlic cloves, squished or grated
thumb-sized piece of fresh ginger, peeled and finely grated
1 tsp ground turmeric
2 tsp ground cinnamon
2 tsp ground cumin
½ tsp ground white pepper
large handful of dried sultanas or cranberries, roughly chopped
2 mugfuls of brown Basmati rice (about 500g), rinsed in cold water
2 litres Baby-friendly bone broth (see p.119) or salt-free vegetable bouillon/stock

Yoghurt topping

¼ cucumber, grated
6 tbsp plain thick Greek yoghurt

WHAT DO I DO?

- In a large frying pan, heat 4 tbsps of the olive oil over a medium heat. While it's heating up, in a small bowl toss the sliced onion in the flour. Once it's all coated, tip the onion pieces into the hot pan and stir for 2 minutes until the onion is browned and crisp. Transfer the onion to a plate lined with paper towels and leave to cool. This is your crispy topping for the grown-up portion.
- Wipe the pan clean and return it to the heat with 4 more tbsps of olive oil. Add the diced onion and stir. As it begins to soften, add the garlic, ginger, turmeric, cinnamon, cumin and pepper. Cook for a minute, stirring often, before adding the dried fruit and rice. Stir to coat the rice in the spiced mixture before pouring in the stock/broth. Put a lid on the pan and reduce the heat to low. Leave to simmer for 18–20 minutes, checking every so often in case the pan needs more liquid.
- When the time's up, stir well and taste to check the rice is soft, then remove the pan from the heat and leave to stand for 5 minutes. Use this time to mix your grated cucumber with your yoghurt, and set the table.
- Remove the pan lid and portion out your baby's meal (fork-mashing the rice a little if your baby prefers a softer texture), spooning a bit of the yoghurt mix on top. Now scatter the crispy fried onions across the surface of the pan and place it on the dining table with the cucumber yoghurt. If you like things spicy, a scattering of finely diced green chilli is a welcome addition.

Chilli con carne

Rich, smoky and flavoursome, this robust dinner does a great job of providing protein and fibre, along with essential minerals like iron. Serve with plain yoghurt, a sprinkle of grated cheese and a side of Baby guac (see p.72). Leftovers can be topped with mashed sweet potato and oven-baked to create a colourful twist on the traditional shepherd's pie.

FOR 2 ADULTS + 2 LITTLE ONES

WHAT DO I NEED?

2 tbsp olive oil
2 red onions, finely diced
2 garlic cloves, squished or grated
2 tsp paprika
2 tsp ground cumin
12 tbsp minced beef (about 180g)
1 × 400g can kidney beans/ black beans, drained
1 × 400g can plum tomatoes
2 mugfuls of cold water, Baby-friendly bone broth (see p.119) or salt-free bouillon/stock

WHAT DO I DO?

- In a shallow, wide pan heat the olive oil and add the red onion. Soften over a medium heat for 3 minutes before adding the garlic, paprika and cumin. Stir to combine, then add the minced beef. Stir continuously for 5 minutes, breaking down the meat with your spoon so it browns all over and combines thoroughly with the other ingredients.
- Now add the beans, stirring and pressing to break them down a little, and the canned tomatoes, again breaking them with your spoon. Splash in the cold water/hot broth/stock and bring to a gentle simmer. Allow to cook for 6–7 minutes, stirring often.
- Remove from the heat, allow to cool, then serve.
- Depending on where you are with teeth, you could fork-mash, blend or serve straight-up. Younger babies will enjoy the chilli with a bit of plain yoghurt and perhaps a spoonful of Baby guac (see p.72). Older babies might like theirs with some boiled brown rice too, to make a more substantial meal.

Brazilian baby jackets

I got chatting with the Brazilian food truck girls in the park one day and they told me how their mamas used to give them sweet potatoes baked whole in their jackets. I'd never thought of baking one like that so I gave it a spin and the baby nearly ate the plate as well as the potato. Sweet potato is a great source of easily digestible dietary fibre along with slow-release carbohydrate and minerals you don't see every day like copper and manganese, plus vitamins C, E and A. Avocado is an all-round nutritional powerhouse, and the beans and dairy are our protein sources.

FOR 2 ADULTS + 2 LITTLE ONES

WHAT DO I NEED?

4 small sweet potatoes
8 tbsp canned black beans (120g)
1 small, ripe avocado
3 tbsp grated Cheddar
1½ tbsp plain yoghurt
a few coriander leaves, snipped or chopped finely

WHAT DO I DO?

- Preheat the oven to 200°C/fan 180°C/Gas mark 6 and bake the sweet potatoes whole for 1 hour.
- Warm and fork-mash the black beans. Fork-mash the avocado. Open the jackets and heap in the beans and grated cheese, wiggling everything about to melt the cheese. Top each with the plain yoghurt, mashed avo and a sprinkle of coriander.
- Give your baby wedges of the potato to hold and explore (skin-on to make it grippy) and/or help them eat this with a spoon.

Magic pizza

A revelation of a recipe that has become a favourite with the YG community. The magic ingredient is gram flour – ground chickpeas. I found a bag for a pound in our local Indian grocer, where I buy bags of spices much more cheaply than at the supermarket, and decided to see what I could make with it. This pizza's so tasty. Vital stats: more protein than an omelette, no refined white flour, no dough-proving, no kneading, no rolling, no scary high cooking temperatures needed to get it crispy. It can take all sorts of toppings and being soft, crisp and gooey all at once, the slices are easy enough for little hands to pick up and grip. This makes six little pizzas about 10cm in diameter = a couple of baby meals, plus a a few for the parents.

FOR 2 ADULTS + 2 LITTLE ONES

WHAT DO I NEED?

10 tbsp gram flour
240–300ml cold water
olive oil
12 cherry tomatoes, diced
1 raw courgette, grated
large handful of grated Cheddar
1 tsp dried oregano

WHAT DO I DO?

- Sift the flour into a mixing bowl, ideally one with a pouring lip (it's important to sift this stuff to remove lumps). Add the water gradually and whisk with a small whisk or fork, stopping when you have a pourable batter.
- Pour a 10cm circle of batter into a frying pan that's been heated up with a generous splash of olive oil. Fry for 60 seconds or so then flip, cooking the pizza base until it's golden on both sides. Transfer onto a baking tray and repeat using the rest of the batter.
- Scatter all the bakes with the diced tomato, grated courgette and Cheddar. Load them as generously as you like. Add a pinch of dried oregano and a squiggle of olive oil over the top, then slide the baking tray under a hot grill for a couple of minutes – long enough for the toppings to go golden, but not so long that the pizza's edges burns. Slice and serve immediately.

Provençal lentils

A fail-safe dinner for evenings when you aren't able to watch the pot. The idea for this one-pot wonder came from our local greengrocer. He grew up in the South of France and talked me through this childhood dish one afternoon when I ran into his shop to escape the torrential rain. The core ingredients are basic, but this dinner punches well above its weight. Lentils are a powerful source of protein. Carrots are packed with vitamin A (they really do help you see in the dark as vitamin A magically boosts the cornea's powers ... useful for nocturnal babies). Onion brings fibre, vitamins B6 and K, calcium and magnesium. Garlic brings antioxidants and the minerals iron, copper and selenium, while courgette adds more dietary fibre, useful for the baby's digestion. We've had other hits with lentils (see p.99 for Gentle lentil dhal), but this time the flavours are a bit punchier and the texture's less creamy. These are lentils, French-gourmet style.

FOR 2 ADULTS + 2 LITTLE ONES

WHAT DO I NEED?

2 onions, diced
2 garlic cloves, squished or grated
2 carrots, diced
2 courgettes, diced
2 tsp dried mixed herbs
8 tbsp green lentils
4 mugfuls of cold water, Baby-friendly bone broth (see box) or salt-free bouillon/stock

WHAT DO I DO?

- Sweat the onion in a small pan with the garlic until soft and translucent, about 4 minutes. Add the carrot, courgette and dried herbs. Stir the veg for a couple of minutes to soften, then add the green lentils (that you have pre-rinsed in water) and your chosen cooking liquid.
- Bring to a gentle simmer, stirring every now and then until the lentils are soft, about 20 minutes. Fork-mash to the right texture for your babe and serve by spoon.

Bone broth

You've probably read about bone broth. 'Boiling your bones' is the culinary act du jour. But why? And why is bone broth appearing in a baby recipe book? Because it's so nutritious. Bone broth might feel like quite an extreme thing to make, but one batch of this will provide a mineral-rich, protein-rich, taste-packed base for all sorts of baby dishes for weeks to come. It's a natural replacement for stock cubes or flavourings and is an easy way to dial up the mineral load in dishes like stews, curries, pot roasts and pasta sauces. Some parents also offer a small amount of bone broth to their babies as a warm drink in between milk feeds, particularly in winter.

It's really just a slow stovetop recipe – biggest pot, 1kg pasture-fed beef bones from the butcher, covered with enough cold water to completely cover – around 2 litres. Add 2 tbsps apple cider vinegar and leave to stand for half an hour, lid on. Turn the heat on and bring to a gentle simmer for 3 hours, checking the water level once or twice and adding a mugful extra if needed. Allow to cool slightly, then remove the bones to the bin, pour the liquid through a sieve into a jug, and store in ice-cube trays in the freezer or sealed jars in the fridge. It will keep for 3 days in the fridge (it will solidify like jelly, but don't worry, just cook with it as usual) and 3 months in the freezer.

Lamb kofta lollipops

The word 'kofta' comes from an old Persian word meaning 'to grind', and ground, spiced lamb dishes remain a delicacy right across the Middle East. This dish works really well as a sharing meal: the grown-ups can have their koftas with big salads, salty olives and crisp toasted pittas, and the baby can have kofta lollipops with a cool, creamy dip for dunking. There's a lot of protein in the lamb and Greek yoghurt. Red onion and cucumber bring fibre, plus vitamins C, K and B1, potassium, phosphorus and magnesium. Cumin adds beautiful aromatic depth, and parsley is more than a flavouring herb – it's a powerhouse of vitamins.

FOR 2 ADULTS + 2 LITTLE ONES

WHAT DO I NEED?

Koftas

dash of olive oil
2 red onions, finely diced
3 tsp ground cumin
12 tbsp minced lamb (180g)
3 garlic cloves, squished or grated
handful parsley leaves, well chopped

Yoghurt dip

½ cucumber, grated
6 tbsp plain Greek yoghurt

WHAT DO I DO?

- Throw all the kofta ingredients into a mixing bowl and with a big spoon or clean hands combine everything together to create your kofta mix. Now (with both hands … but only for a minute!) form little handfuls of the mixture around little wooden skewers (that have been soaked for 10 mins) or around metal teaspoons.
- Wearing an oven glove, lay the spoons onto your grill and cook under a medium grill for 3–4 minutes before carefully turning them (with the oven glove) to gently cook on the other side. If it's the summertime, these are fantastic cooked on the BBQ.
- Meanwhile, grate the cucumber on a box grater and mix with a Greek yoghurt to create the dip.
- Once you're happy that the lamb is cooked through, allow the meat to cool to a safe temperature, either take the meat off the skewer (if sharp) or wipe the spoon handles clean and serve up a lollipop to your babe with the dunking dip.

Serve the lollipops and yoghurt dip with bowls of Baby hummus (see p.68), Baba-ganoush (see p.69) and a warm Stovetop flatbread (see p.83).

Mini Moroccan tagine

A few years ago, when B was just a twinkle in her dad's eye, he and I travelled to Marrakech for a wedding. It was magical – a big party in the desert with whispering palm trees, bubbling water fountains, smoky incense and a sunset (and a bride) so beautiful it'd bring a little tear to your eye. Less magical was the headache the next morning. The only thing I remember with certainty was the tagine we ate. It was one of those simple, incredible meals you'll never forget – everything about it was perfect.

This seems like an ambitious thing to feed a baby, but really it's super simple to make and very easy to eat. It's a longer ingredient list here than we're used to, but I promise it's worth it for those mesmerising North African flavours.

FOR 2 ADULTS + 2 LITTLE ONES

WHAT DO I NEED?

1 tbsp olive or coconut oil
1 red onion, diced
2 garlic cloves, squished or grated
2 carrots, grated
2 courgettes, grated
8 tbsp drained canned chickpeas
1 butternut squash, diced
4 tomatoes, fresh or canned
2 tsp ground cumin
2 tsp ground cinnamon
2 Medjool dates, diced
360ml cold water, Baby-friendly bone broth (see p.119) or salt-free bouillon/stock
4 tsp plain yoghurt, to serve

WHAT DO I DO?

- Heat up a pan, adding the olive or coconut oil. Throw in the diced onion and garlic. Sweat for a couple of minutes before piling in the grated carrots, courgettes, chickpeas, squash and tomatoes. Follow with the spices and dates. Pour in the water, broth or stock. Stir, lid, and simmer gently for 12–15 mins, checking the pan halfway through and adding a splash more water if you think it's needed.
- Remove from the heat, allow to cool, pop in a bowl and then mash or whizz, depending on where you're babies at with teeth.
- Very nice with a blob of yoghurt on top, and you can make this a more substantial meal by serving it over wholemeal cous cous, which cooks in seconds.

Add diced lamb to up the protein and mineral content, though the chickpeas and butternut do a very good nutritional job by themselves.

Salmon fishcakes with tartare dip

These are clever little fishcakes: the pretty pink salmon delivers quality protein as well as omega 3 fatty acids (such as DHA that helps with brain function and vision), vitamin D and various B-vits and minerals phosphorus, selenium and potassium. And the broccoli and potato provide dietary fibre, vitamin C, plus a bit of iron and calcium. There's also calcium in the tartare sauce, along with a very interesting piquant flavour. There's evidence to suggest that a lot of weaning babies are very receptive to tastes on the bitter/sour spectrum, so here's a way to offer that kind of flavour in a quick and easy dinner.

FOR 2 ADULTS + 2 LITTLE ONES

WHAT DO I NEED?

Fishcakes

2 fillets of salmon, skin on
8 new potatoes, halved
small broccoli head, broken into florets
2 tsp butter
olive oil or butter

Dip

4 cornichons/slice of pickled cucumber, rinsed of pickling vinegar
8 pickled capers, rinsed of pickling vinegar
4 tsp plain yoghurt

WHAT DO I DO?

- Steam the salmon (skin on) and broccoli trees over a pan of boiling water, cooking the potatoes in the water underneath. This means you can cook everything in one go; they should take about 8–10 minutes depending on how steamy things get (you can hack a stove-top steamer by placing a metal sieve over a pan of simmering water, with a pan lid on top of the sieve).
- Once the ingredients are cooked through, skin the fish and fork-mash the potatoes. Put in a bowl, breaking up the cooked broccoli heads on top. Fork-mash everything together, then wet your hands and get squishing. Form fishcakes using a couple of teaspoons of mixture for each.
- Place in a frying pan that's hot with a little olive oil or butter, you may need to cook these in batches. Fry and flip the fishcakes for 30 seconds each side (the ingredients are already cooked so this stage is quick). Once crisp and golden, remove to a plate and cool slightly before serving as finger-food.
- While they're cooling, make your tartare dip. Finely chop the pickle or pickled cucumber and smash the capers with a knife, then combine with the yoghurt.

There's evidence to suggest that a lot of weaning babies are very receptive to tastes on the bitter/sour spectrum, so here's a way to offer that kind of flavour in a quick and easy dinner.

Rainbow ragu

No baby cookbook would be complete without a spag bol recipe and here's mine. It's up to you whether you serve this with wholewheat (or spelt) spaghetti, or make your own crazy ribbons of courgetti (using nothing more fancy than your vegetable peeler). Top them off with a seriously tasty sauce that hits it out of the park nutritionally: iron, protein, fibre, minerals, plus heaps of vitamin C, which helps the baby's digestive system absorb that all-important iron.

FOR 2 ADULTS + 2 LITTLE ONES

WHAT DO I NEED?

a splash of olive oil
1 onion, diced
8 mushrooms, diced
2 garlic cloves, squished or grated
12 tbsp minced beef (about 180g)
½ tsp dried oregano
1 × 400g can of plum tomatoes
2 carrots, grated
300ml cold water, Baby-friendly bone broth (see p.119) or salt-free bouillon/stock

To serve

200g wholewheat/spelt spaghetti strands, snapped in half
OR
3 courgettes, sliced lengthways and made into ribbons with your vegetable peeler

WHAT DO I DO?

- Add a splash of olive oil to a pan and soften the onion, mushroom and garlic for a few minutes. When the onion has become soft and translucent, add the minced beef and oregano. Brown the meat for 5 minutes, stirring regularly.
- Add the tomatoes, carrots and bone broth/stock/water. Bash the tomatoes with your spoon as you stir, and leave to simmer for 8 minutes, stirring regularly.
- If you're cooking pasta, cook it now while the sauce is simmering. If you're using courgetti, once the sauce has simmered for 7 minutes, mix in the raw courgetti, put a lid on the pan and leave it for a minute or two. The sauce will warm the courgette so it's soft enough to eat, but firm enough for a baby to pick up.
- Let your baby attack this dish with their hands and a spoon or quickly whizz it smooth in the blender.

This sauce freezes brilliantly, so scale up and stash some portions in the freezer. Adults should add a little salt, Parmesan and chilli to theirs.

Popcorn chicken + rainbow root fries

Inspired by the local pop-up buttermilk fried chicken shack, this is both fun and simple … and though it feels like a real treat, it's very nutritious. Good-quality lean protein in the chicken, encased in the good fats, fibre and minerals of the almonds. With a side order of slow-release-carbohydrate-rich root fries. Chicken and chips for a weaning baby? Sure!

FOR 2 ADULTS + 2 LITTLE ONES

WHAT DO I NEED?

400g skin-on root vegetables, sliced into batons (carrot, parsnip, potato, sweet potato or beetroot)
6 tbsp coconut oil
3 eggs, beaten
12 tbsp ground almonds
3 chicken breasts, diced into 4–5 small cubes
splash of olive oil

WHAT DO I DO?

- Preheat the oven to 200°C/fan 180°C/Gas mark 6.
- Place the baby-fist-sized slices of root veg in a roasting tray and add the coconut oil. Place in the oven for 45–60 minutes.
- Meanwhile, line up three bowls. Crack the egg into the first one and whisk. Add almonds to the second and leave the third empty.
- Take a cube of chicken and dunk it in the egg, then roll it in the almonds, coating on all sides. Place in the final bowl and do the rest.
- To cook, either bake for 7–8 minutes, turning once, or fry in a splash of olive oil for 3–4 minutes, moving the pieces around in the pan regularly to encourage even cooking. Once your pieces are golden and toasty, cut one in half and check the meat, ensuring it's thoroughly cooked. You may need to cook these in batches.
- Leave to cool slightly before serving up alongside the fries. Quick, tasty and nutritious finger food for your baby to explore. Or fling.

Malaysian coconut fish curry

If you follow YG on Instagram you'll know about Baby B's thing for curry. She's famous for it at nursery, and any time she's under the weather or teething, a bowl of curry seems to turn her frown upside down.

This coconut-y version sees protein, carbohydrate and fats well-represented along with many, many vitamins and minerals. It'd take me longer to write them all down than it'll take you to cook this. The coconut milk alone contains practically every essential micronutrient a growing baby needs, including a compound called lauric acid, which is rare in nature but abundant in breastmilk. No wonder babies like coconut! The garlic, turmeric, cinnamon and cumin are packed with minerals and antioxidants. In fact, in certain ancient food cultures all four of these ingredients are held up as sacred health-giving power foods. Amen to that. This dish is lovely by itself or served over super-quick, fibre-rich cauliflower rice, but any variety of brown rice is an excellent accompaniment, too.

The first proper meal Baby B ever had was a curry and ever since, she gets leg-waggly for anything spicy and aromatic.

FOR 2 ADULTS + 2 LITTLE ONES

WHAT DO I NEED?

1 onion, diced
2 garlic cloves, squished or grated
splash of olive oil
¼ tsp ground turmeric
¼ tsp ground cumin
¼ tsp ground cinnamon
2 sweet potatoes, peeled and cubed
1 × 400g can chickpeas, rinsed
4 mugfuls of cold water
3 fillets of any firm white fish, skinned and cut into cubes
1 × 400ml can coconut milk

Cauliflower rice (optional)

1 cauliflower
4 tbsp cold water
little olive oil

WHAT DO I DO?

- Soften the onion and garlic in a splash of olive oil in the bottom of a saucepan. Add the three dry spices and sweet potato cubes and chickpeas, stirring to coat everything, before adding the cold water. Lid on. Simmer for 15 minutes.
- Meanwhile, grate the raw cauliflower on a box grater to create cauliflower 'rice'. Tip the grated cauli and cold water into a warm frying pan with a little olive oil and heat for 6–7 minutes, stirring occasionally.
- Turning your attention back to the curry, scatter in the cubes of fish and coconut milk and re-lid for 4 minutes. The fish will steam-cook and take on the curry's colour and flavour. Remove the curry from the heat, allow to cool slightly, then serve or mash/whizz to a smoother texture.
- Serve the curry over come cauliflower rice or boiled brown rice. Oh, and wear a bib (maybe both of you …). Turmeric is magic stuff, but it doesn't half stain.

Pho boodles

'Fuuuu'. 'Fuu'. What's that, Baby B? You fancy some of those vibey Viet soup noodles everyone's slurping on? PHO-k! Pho noodles (pronounced 'fuu', not 'foh', well done little B you were right) are everywhere now. The basis of any good pho bowl is the broth (find my recipe on p.119). As well as the mineral goodness of the broth, here we have vegetables bringing vitamins C and A, plus slow-release carb for sustained energy, spices ginger and garlic providing essential minerals and environmental-damage-fighting antioxidants ... and the nutritious buckwheat is back! If you don't have buckwheat noodles to hand, spiralize some raw butternut squash. No spiralizer, no problem; use a vegetable peeler instead.

FOR 2 ADULTS + 2 LITTLE ONES

WHAT DO I NEED?

4 thin slices of fresh ginger
1 garlic clove, squished/grated
4 mugfuls of Baby-friendly bone broth (see p.119) or salt-free bouillon/stock
2 carrots, grated
8 small mushrooms, grated
small broccoli head, broken into florets
200g dried buckwheat noodles
OR
1 butternut squash, spiralized or peeled into thin shreds
4 hard-boiled eggs, to serve (optional)

WHAT DO I DO?

- Simmer the fresh ginger and the squished garlic clove in the broth or stock. Add the carrots, mushrooms and broccoli. Allow the veg to soften before adding the buckwheat noodles, snapped in half, or your homemade butternut noodles.
- Bring to a gentle simmer for 6–7 minutes, stirring occasionally. If you're adding any fish or chicken, slice it up and put it into the cooking liquid now to poach. Chopped hard-boiled egg can be scattered on top of the dish after it's cooked.
- Once everything is cooked and soft, fish out the ginger slice and discard. Serve up as it comes – the baby can slurp the liquid and grab pieces of everything else, or this dish is easy to pulse in the blender and serve by spoon. Maybe reserve a few pieces of vegetable to pick up and play with.

The noodles are a good protein source (about 14g/100g) but this is even better if you add chicken, salmon or finely chopped hard-boiled egg.

Magic hacks on timeless childhood indulgences like ice cream, lollies, biscuits, cake balls, sweets and puddings, without a grain of the white stuff in sight.

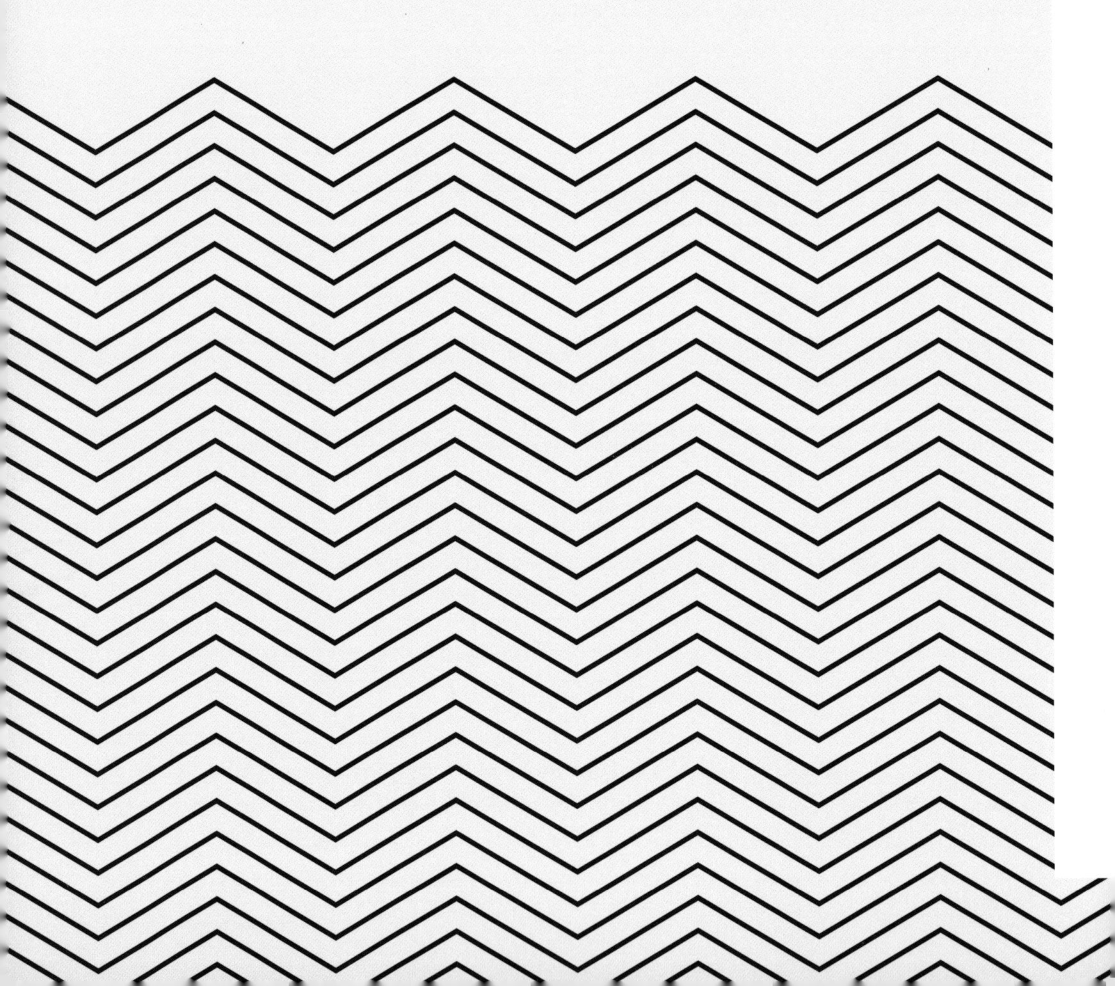

Puddings, cakes + sweet bakes

It's practically impossible to be a parent these days without being aware of the sugar debate – there's a story about the perils of sugar in the news almost every day. While naturally occurring sugars (like those in fresh fruit) are considered an entirely safe and desirable part of your baby's diet as they bring with them a host of vitamins, minerals and fibre, the same is not true of refined sugar.

Refined sugar – extracted from plants and formulated into granules or syrups – is now known to be at best nutritionally useless and, at worst, addictive and health-damaging. It's frustratingly difficult to avoid (or even keep track of). It has many names and shows up in unexpected places – even in foods that you'd assume were savoury, like pasta sauces and crisps. The British government recently took the unprecedented step of implementing a tax levy on sugary drinks. Governments don't do that sort of thing without good reason. Keeping your baby away from refined sugar is more difficult than it should be but it's not impossible, and it doesn't mean taking a joyless attitude to treats.

One-ingredient ice cream

Imagine the scene. Hottest day of the year, nearly 30°C in the shade in old London town. One of those days when people try and fry eggs on the pavement ... and succeed. Well, of course this was the day B started teething like crazy. Pink-eyed and sad, she could barely close her mouth for the pain. Nothing seemed to help. Until this. I was vaguely aware of the Instagram craze for 'N-ice Cream', but this flaming-hot day my Insta-feed was flooded with the stuff so I gave it a go. I froze up some banana slices and was amazed to whizz them into soft, creamy peaks that'd make Mr. Whippy weep. And somehow there's no overpowering banana-y taste. Needless to say, B loved it and gave the first smile of the day. Try it, mamas, teething or not – why should babies miss out on important food trends because they're too little to monitor hashtags?

FOR 2 ADULTS + 2 LITTLE ONES

WHAT DO I NEED?

2 ripe bananas, thinly sliced and frozen
a splash or two of cold water or your baby's usual milk
optional flavours: strawberries, raspberries, blueberries, unsweetened cacao, cinnamon or nut butter

We've gone to town here to create the old 'Neapolitan' three-flavour combo of my childhood, making up three mini batches – one plain, one with a strawberry and the third with a pinch of unsweetened cacao. But this ice cream is a canvas for many flavours: cinnamon (anti-inflammatory, antioxidants), raspberries/ blueberries (vitamin C, fibre, antioxidants) or creamy smooth nut butter (vitamin E, protein, good fats).

WHAT DO I DO?

- Tip the frozen banana slices into your blender with the water/milk. Pulse, stop, look, give the blender cup a shake. Keep going, pulse by pulse, and after 45–60 seconds of whizzing, maybe less, you'll be left with a creamy soft-scoop texture.
- Serve IMMEDIATELY. If you're adding flavours, throw them in at the start.

Sweet potato cookies

Weaning cookies. No, really. Easy, quick and inexpensive, all we need is a few basic store cupboard ingredients. Sweet potato is full of fibre, slow-release carb and all sorts of vitamins and minerals, notably vitamin A, which is thought to support the development of the eye. Egg brings the protein, and the potato's sweetness is enhanced by natural aromatics cinnamon and vanilla. A batch will keep in the fridge for 3 days and you can warm them in the oven ahead of serving.

MAKES 12 COOKIES

WHAT DO I NEED?

1 large sweet potato or 2 small ones
8 tbsp oats
4 tsp coconut oil or butter, softened or melted
1 egg
1 tsp ground cinnamon
2 tsp vanilla extract

WHAT DO I DO?

- Preheat the oven to 200°C/fan 180°C/Gas mark 6. Peel, cube and steam the sweet potato.
- Leave to cool to room temperature, uncovered so the steam escapes and dries out the potato slightly.
- Into your blender go the oats. Whizz them to powder, then add the cooled sweet potato cubes, coconut oil/butter, egg, cinnamon and vanilla. Whizz to blend.
- Drop 12 circles of the mixture on a coconut oil/butter-greased baking tray, then bake for 12–15 minutes until they're golden at edges, but still soft in the centre. Remove to a wire tray to cool.

Blueberry muffins

What is life without cake? I have no idea because since having a baby, I never seem to be far from one, and now we have recipes like this, neither is Baby B. She loves these served up warm with a cold drink of milk. Sweet, squidgy, crispy and tart all at once, these muffins are a dead-ringer for the blueberry muffins at our local coffee shop. Except no sugar, only banana. They put coconut in theirs … and now so do we.

MAKES 5–6 BIG OR 12 MINI

WHAT DO I NEED?

6 tbsp oats
2 tbsp desiccated coconut
2 ripe bananas, mashed very smooth
3 tbsp coconut oil
1 tsp vanilla extract
1 tsp baking powder
15–20 blueberries, chopped in half

WHAT DO I DO?

- Preheat the oven to 200°C/fan 180°C/Gas mark 6. Whizz the oats in a blender until you have flour. Tip into a bowl with the coconut, mashed banana, coconut oil, vanilla extract and baking powder. Lastly, throw in the sliced blueberries. Mix well with a big spoon then divide into a well-greased muffin tin (or use paper muffin cases). This mixture will make 12 mini muffins or 5–6 regular-sized.
- Bake for 20 mins (mini muffins) or 25 mins (regular).
- Allow to cool to a safe temperature, then serve … these make a great afternoon snack. Store in an airtight container/cake tin for 3 days.

Baby bliss balls, three ways

Holy cake balls, these are good. Free of refined sugar, these baby-safe versions of those vibey bliss balls that you see in the trendy cafés are *almost* too good to be true. Quick, easy and cheap, they're the perfect anytime-anywhere baby snack: easy to grip and not horrendously messy, they travel well and keep brilliantly for 3 days in the fridge (if the daddies don't find them). And because these balls are raw, we don't lose any nutrients through applying heat during cooking.

Paradise balls

All the tropical vibes in one little ball. Banana and coconut bring fibre, carbohydrate and a host of vitamins and minerals, notably vitamin C and potassium. Ground almonds are easy to digest, full of vitamin E and beautiful good fats. It's a tree nut so of course approach with some caution in case of allergies, however it's one of the lowest-allergy risks of them all.

MAKES 12–16 BALLS

WHAT DO I NEED?

1 banana
4 tbsp ground almonds
6 tbsp desiccated coconut
+ extra for dusting

WHAT DO I DO?

- Fork-mash the banana in a bowl (if you're #OneHandCooking, rest the bowl on a tea towel so it doesn't slip). Scatter in the almonds and coconut. Stir until you have a soft dough.
- Rest the mixture in the fridge for 5 mins, then it's time to roll.
- Take the chilled bowl to the playmat and let the baby watch you make the balls (= eat half the mixture). This amount should yield about twelve or sixteen pram-snack-sized balls.
- Finish by rolling them in an extra bit of coconut for grip: put some coconut in a teacup and whizz each ball round until they are covered. Endless baby LOLs.

These baby-safe versions of those vibey bliss balls that you see in the trendy cafés are almost too good to be true.

Raw carrot cake balls

As well as digestion-supporting fibre, raw carrot contains loads of vitamin A in all that orange beta carotene ... nature's food colouring. Also vitamins C, K and B8, plus copper and iron. Almonds pack good fats and vit E, and the dates bring natural sweetness along with pretty much all the other essential vitamins and minerals. Nutmeg, cinnamon and vanilla dial up the CAKE flavour.

MAKES 12–16 BALLS

WHAT DO I NEED?

1 carrot, grated (leave the skin on)
4 soft dates, stones removed and roughly torn up
¼ tsp vanilla extract
¼ tsp ground nutmeg
¼ tsp ground cinnamon
6 tbsp ground almonds + extra for dusting

WHAT DO I DO?

- Put the grated carrot into your blender with the torn-up dates, vanilla, nutmeg and cinnamon. Pulse several times to break down the dates and carrot, then tip the smooth, blended mixture into a bowl and stir in the almonds.
- When a soft, sticky dough forms, ditch the spoon and go in with clean hands, gently forming balls – the mixture should yield twelve or sixteen depending on exact size.
- Roll the balls, one by one, around and around in a teacup that's been scattered with a bit of ground almond. This will coat all the sides of the cake balls, making them grippy instead of sticky.

Raspberry ripple balls

These remind me of the 'coconut ice' I used to eat as a teenager – a sort of soft nougat made from desiccated coconut that was popular in 1990s Britain. There were pink and white versions, and I loved both. These all-natural balls bring together coconut and raspberry to make a pretty, swirly ripple effect.

MAKES 12–16 BALLS

WHAT DO I NEED?
8 tbsp desiccated coconut
8 tbsp ground almonds
4 tbsp cashew butter
2 tbsp coconut oil
¼ vanilla extract
zest of ½ lemon
4 fresh raspberries

WHAT DO I DO?
• Put everything but the raspberries in a mixing bowl and with clean hands (or just one if the other is full of baby), squeeze and combine everything together.
• When you have a soft dough, fork-mash the raspberries and mix them gently through the dough to create rough swirls.
• Roll the balls between your palms, dusting each in a little extra desiccated coconut for grip, using the teacup-swirling trick.

Chocolate truffles

Sometimes you just need chocolate. I had a craving the first night I solo-parented Baby B. Her eyes had finally closed and I'd commando-rolled out of the room, tiptoeing downstairs, only to find the cupboard was bare. I was marooned.
In desperation I opened the pantry and used what I had to make a plate of super decadent, squidgy chocolate truffles. They're even better than the real thing. This recipe yields 12–14 sweets, and spares will keep in a small airtight jar in the fridge for 5 days. Add texture by rolling your truffles in desiccated coconut or crushed pistachios instead of cacao. Or add orange zest to your mixture for a choc-orange effect.

MAKES 12–14 TRUFFLES

WHAT DO I NEED?

2 Medjool dates
2 tbsp smooth almond butter
2 tsp cacao
1 tsp vanilla extract
2–3 tbsp ground almonds
splash of cold water

WHAT DO I DO?

- Blend all the ingredients together in blender until you have a sticky dough.
- With clean hands, take fat pinches of the mixture and roll between your palms to create truffles.
- One by one, put them into a teacup that you've scattered an extra bit of cacao or ground almonds into and whizz the truffles round and round to coat them. Now the truffles are grippy rather than sticky.

Baby-friendly banana bread

Banana bread is my absolute favourite, and this version's so nice you won't miss the granulated sugar. Cinnamon brings depth and aromatic sweetness. And buckwheat flour is especially nutritious. Coconut oil is our fat here. I don't have enough space to extol the virtues of this stuff for your baby, but try cooking with it if you haven't. And rub a bit on your baby's skin, and into your own hair. It's a wonder.

MAKES 1 LOAF OR 6 MUFFINS

WHAT DO I NEED?

2 regular bananas, mashed smooth
4 tbsp coconut oil, melted
2 eggs
4 tbsp buckwheat flour
2 tsp ground cinnamon

Buckwheat is a bit harder to find than regular flour, but it's a worthy investment as it's so nutritious and versatile (pancakes, muffins, banana bread, biscuits). It behaves just like standard refined white flour, so there are no surprises.

WHAT DO I DO?

- Preheat the oven to 200°C/fan 180°C/Gas mark 6. In a mixing bowl, stir together your mashed banana, melted coconut oil and eggs. Fold in the flour and cinnamon, blending well with a big spoon.
- Spoon into a muffin tray or small loaf tin and bake for 15–20 minutes until the cake's surface is golden and a metal skewer or knife plunged into the cake comes out clean, rather than coated in wet mixture. Leave the cake to cool entirely to room temperature before serving.
- The texture of this cake improves mightily as it cools – it becomes denser, but somehow sweeter and altogether more satisfying. OK, so it's not as sweet as the local bakery's version ... but if your babe's anything like mine, s/he's already waaay sweet enough.
- Great as a pudding or afternoon treat with a splodge of Superbaby superjam (see p.152) or stashed in your pram bag for an on-the-go snack.

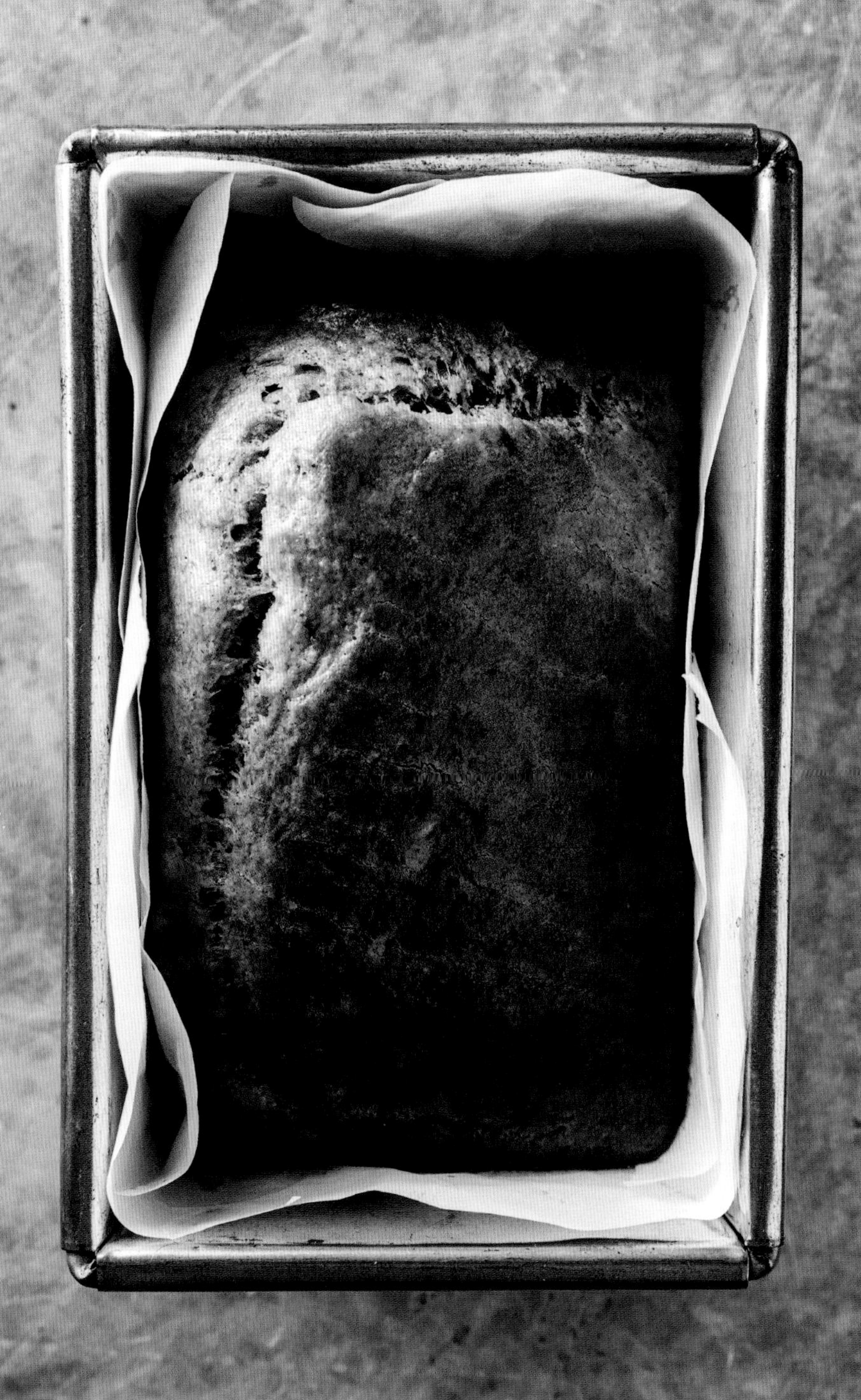

Superbaby superjam

Jam. For babies? No way. Way! A jar of shop-bought jam can contain as much as 60–70 percent sugar. So this nutrient-packed, multi-purpose jam is a revelation. The only sugar it contains is what's naturally present in the strawberries. It requires no cooking and will keep for a week in the fridge.

It's all down to one magic ingredient: chia seeds. B's dad and I had been sprinkling these ancient South American wonder seeds on our breakfasts, soups and smoothies for a while but WHO KNEW how excellent chias are for babies? Fibre. Calcium. Magnesium. Manganese. Phosphorous. Pretty much the richest plant-based source of omega 3 fatty acids. They pack an almighty nutrient punch, and are tasteless and tiny – no choking risk. This jam works with all sorts of fruits, and adding seasonal spices is lovely. The original and best, though, is simple strawberry flavour. Why? Strawberries are incredibly rich in vitamins C and A and bring a wealth of antioxidants, along with rare minerals including copper.

MAKES 350G

WHAT DO I NEED?

1 punnet of strawberries (150–200g)
4 tsp chia seeds
splash of vanilla extract
zest of ¼ lemon

WHAT DO I DO?

- Tip the cleaned and hulled strawberries into a blender. Whizz them until smooth, then add the seeds, vanilla and lemon zest. Blend again, for a few seconds, then pour the liquid into an old glass jar (I use old nut butter jars that have been through the dishwasher). Lid on and into the fridge. Leave for a couple of hours.
- The seeds will absorb liquid from the fruit pulp and swell to form a soft-set jam that's a beautiful addition to any baby breakfast or pudding.
- It's lovely spread onto one of the baby bakes (like the Banana bread, see p.150), as a dip for fresh fruit sticks or as a quick topping for Greek yoghurt or pancakes (see p.56).

This nutrient-packed, multi-purpose jam is a revelation. The only sugar it contains is what's naturally present in the strawberries.

Jammy dodgers (with nothing dodgy)

Who doesn't love a jammy dodger? These cookies are a fun, well-balanced snack, containing protein, carbohydrate, vitamins, minerals and good fats. The ingredients here are simple and easy to find but they're not the cheapest, I know. However, this mix is enough for a batch of 12 and they keep well for 3 days in a sealed box/tin. The jam here is my Superbaby superjam.

MAKES 12 COOKIES

WHAT DO I NEED?

6 tsp coconut oil, softened or melted
6 tsp smooth almond butter (or cashew)
½ banana, mashed smoothly
1 teacup of ground almonds (about 100g)
1 tsp ground cinnamon
pinch of ground ginger
1 tsp vanilla extract
12 tsp Superbaby superjam (see p.152)

WHAT DO I DO?

- Oven on to 200°C/fan 180°C/Gas mark 6. Mix everything together well in a mixing bowl, resting the bowl on a tea towel if you're #OneHandCooking to stop it moving around.
- When you have a thick, sticky dough, take a baking tray greased with a bit of coconut oil and make 12 heaped teaspoon balls of mixture.
- Using cleans hands or a teaspoon, form them into rounds and press a 'well' into the centre of each. That's where the jam will go after they're baked. Bake for 15–20 minutes until the edges are golden.
- Cool to a safe temperature, then add a teaspoon of the jam to each biscuit and serve. They're extra nice when they're still a bit warm.

Chocolate fudgesicles

Do you know anyone who'd be up for a creamy chocolate ice cream treat (with a side of fibre, carb, good plant-based fats, magnesium, potassium, calcium, manganese, copper and iron?) OK then. Before we get into it we need to talk about cacao. It's the raw version of cocoa powder … being raw it's much more nutrient-dense. Some parents avoid cacao/cocoa for their weaning babes in case there are traces of naturally occurring caffeine. That is sensible, although in the quantity we're using here it's not a worry.

MAKES 12 LOLLIES

WHAT DO I NEED?

2 ripe avocados
2 ripe bananas
4 tsp cacao/cocoa
2 Medjool dates, stones removed

WHAT DO I DO?

Blend together all the ingredients to create a smooth mix. Divide the mixture among twelve mini ice lolly moulds or a large ice cube tray. Freeze until solid. Bibs at the ready.

You can soak the dates in boiled water for a few minutes first to help them become extra squidgy.

Pina colada pops

Tropical vibes, summery flavours. These mocktail pops are creamy and sweet with a real zing. The pineapple is packed with vitamin C and dietary fibre and the coconut milk contains a rare and magic ingredient: lauric acid, which is rare in nature but is abundant in human breast milk. It's a fatty acid known to positively affect the baby's immunology and brain development. Clever pina colada pops.

These mocktail pops are creamy and sweet with a real zing.

MAKES 12 LOLLIES

WHAT DO I NEED?

1 fresh pineapple
2 bananas
1 × 400ml can of coconut milk

WHAT DO I DO?

- Blend roughly equal amounts of pineapple, banana and coconut milk. Pulse the blender a few times until you have a smooth mixture, then divide among twelve lolly moulds.
- Freeze for 3 hours, then it's party time.
- Got a bit of leftover mixture ...? Hello, splash of rum. Hello, deckchair. Hello, naptime.

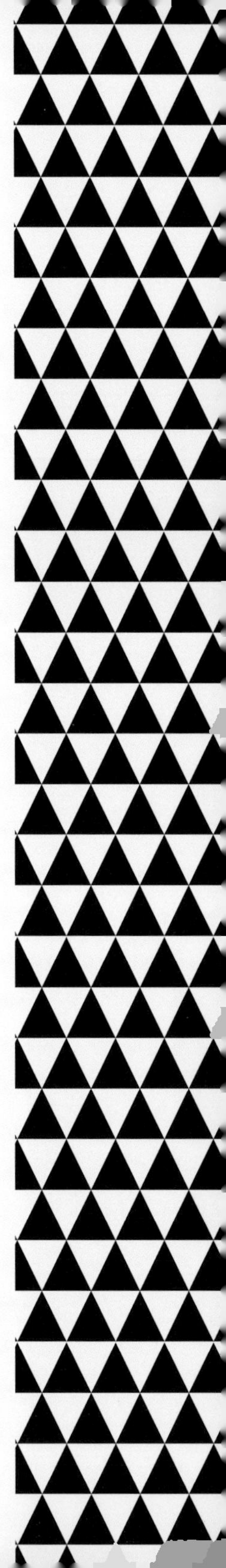

Dip-dye avocado pops

These luxurious, creamy lollies are so good you won't believe they're half-vegetable. An avo is a baby banquet – a feast of nutrients. Protein. The best fats. Minerals and vitamins in pretty staggering quantities. All we're really missing for balance is a carb-source ... enter Mr Banana. This recipe works brilliantly with just these two ingredients, but let's treat the babies to one more: strawberries. Strawberries do rapidly go out of season so if you can't find fresh, use frozen. Strawbs bring a host of vitamins and minerals, and taste as sweet as a summer's day.

MAKES 12 LOLLIES

WHAT DO I NEED?

2 soft avocados
2 ripe bananas
a little cold water (or any milk)
4 strawberries

WHAT DO I DO?

- Scoop the avocados into your blender and break up the bananas on top. Add a little cold water (or any milk). Pulse and whizz.
- Once you have a smooth, thick but pourable texture, pour half of it into your ice lolly moulds.
- Add the strawberries to your blender and whizz. Now you have a pink mix. Use this to fill the twelve lolly moulds.
- Three hours in the freezer and you'll have lovely two-tone, double-flavour lollies.

Yoghurt bark

Fun to make and even more fun to eat, this pick-up-able frozen yoghurt is a revelation, especially if your baby is teething as it soothes angry gums while providing some great nutrition. Protein, fibre and slow-release carb along with all sorts of vitamins and minerals, and no refined sugars, emulsifiers, thickeners, stabilisers, artificial preservatives or other junk. Many combinations of fruit/spices work, but I like this simple classic: a banana-sweetened creamy yoghurt base with a mix of chopped berries.

FOR 2 ADULTS + 2 LITTLE ONES

WHAT DO I NEED?

2 teacups of plain thick Greek yoghurt
½ banana
large handful of chopped soft fruit (strawberries, raspberries, blueberries, blackberries)

WHAT DO I DO?

- Put the yoghurt and banana into your blender and whizz until smooth. Spread into a shallow dish (I use a deep rectangular baking tray to achieve 1cm thickness) that you've lined with clingfilm, and scatter your berries evenly over the top, pressing some in and leaving others on the surface.
- Freeze for 2 hours, then use the clingfilm to lift the bark from the dish and break it up into shards as big or small as you like.
- Spare pieces will keep in the freezer for a month.

If you're concerned about the berry pieces, just whizz the berries into the yoghurt-banana mix to create smooth bark that has the same nutritional goodness.

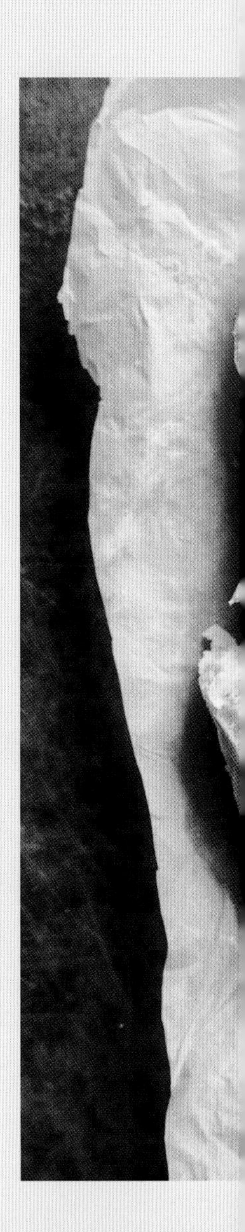

This is the point I bid you farewell for now, and give you a massive high five for everything you've done to help your baby get off on the right foot with eating well.

Party bashes without sugar crashes

Celebrating your baby's first birthday.

If you're reading this page near the beginning of your weaning journey, you probably can't believe the little baby of yours will ever reach the grand old age of one. One is a huge milestone for babies and for their parents. It's also a big developmental stage as far as eating goes. From here on in your baby will begin (if they haven't already!) to have an opinion on what and when they feel like eating, and with a full set of teeth fast approaching, they'll be increasingly able to tackle meals with more independence.

Helping your baby learn to eat of course isn't 'done' yet, far from it, but you've laid powerful groundwork and hopefully have a healthy, happy baby who is curious about food.

Whether you're throwing a big first birthday party or keeping the celebrations to close family, it's nice to mark the occasion with a special celebration table laden with exciting and healthy foods that your baby can enjoy along with everyone else. It's suprisingly easy to create an inviting party scene that even Willy Wonka would be proud of, without reaching for anything sugary or artificial. I'll show you how!

1st birthday cake without refined sugar

When it's time to celebrate, you're gonna need a celebration cake. A squidgy chocolate one, ideally. With no refined sugar, no refined grains, heaps of nutrients and that's no fuss to make. The key ingredients in this one are banana, eggs, unrefined flour, a few dates and cacao powder. So we're looking at a LOT of nutrition in every slice, as well as all that gooey chocolatey goodness. Instead of sugar icing, you can decorate it with non-edibles like a ribbon, big fat sequins, edible glitter, your baby's favourite small toys and, of course, that big '1' candle.

MAKES 1 LARGE CAKE

WHAT DO I NEED?

4 eggs
1 teacup of coconut oil, melted (or softened unsalted butter)
4 tsp vanilla extract
a couple of pinches of ground cinnamon
3 teacups of spelt flour (or you could use wholemeal or buckwheat)
6 tsp cacao powder
2 tsp baking powder/bicarbonate of soda
4 big bananas, mashed very smoothly
8–12 dates, diced
2 teacups of milk, any variety (I use full-fat organic cow's milk)

For the topping

2 teacups whipping, double or heavy cream
1 tsp vanilla extract
sliced fresh fruit

WHAT DO I DO?

- Preheat the oven to 200°C/fan 180°C/Gas mark 6. Grease two small cake tins (I used two 20cm round cake tins).
- Find a standard size teacup to hold about 200ml water. This is your measurer, instead of weighing scales.
- Crack the eggs into a mixing bowl and whisk in the melted coconut oil or butter. Add the vanilla extract and cinnamon. Whisk until pale and a little fluffy.
- Sieve in the flour, cacao powder and baking powder/bicarb, folding the dry goods in gently. Fold the bananas into the batter and mix in the dates. Finish with the milk.
- Pour the mixture into the tins. Place in the oven for 30–35 mins. Check it is cooked by stabbing with a knife or cocktail stick into the centre – if it comes out clean, it is cooked. Let cool completely before sandwiching and topping with well-beaten fresh cream spiked with vanilla extract. Decorate with fruit slices.

Whole cow's milk tastes 100 times nicer than the semi-skimmed I've used for years. And it has a higher nutrient load than lower-fat milks (some of the fat-soluble vitamins are lost when the fat's skimmed off).

Here's the menu we put together for Baby B's bash

Layered-up chia trifle

• Make two batches of chia pudding (see p.54) and layer one batch in the bottom of a transparent trifle dish (so you can see the colourful layers).
• Scatter the pudding with fresh soft and juicy fruits, chopped or squished as you prefer (peach/nectarine, raspberries, strawberries, blueberries, mango).
• Now layer freshly whipped double cream (add a drop or two of vanilla extract).
• Layer your second batch of chia pudding and repeat – a fruit layer and finally, more cream to finish. Decorate the top of your trifle with a little fresh fruit as a garnish. I suggest a little pile right in the centre or a spiral/starburst of coloured fruits.

Baby bliss ball mountain

Make up multiple batches of the three flavours of the Baby bliss balls on p.144 and stack them in layers on a cake stand. Decorate with little fresh flowers.

Chips 'n dips

A platter of Rainbow root fries (see page 130) and cool cucumber sticks arranged around bowls of Baby guac (see p.72) and Traffic light baby hummus (see p.68).

Mama's ice cream parlour

• A couple of days before your party make up a few batches of Pina colada pops (see p.158) and Dip-dye avocado pops (see p.159), removing each finished batch to a box/tray in your freezer to free up lolly moulds.
• Run the frozen lollies under the cold tap to separate any that have stuck together and serve immediately.
• Also freeze up a mega-batch of thinly sliced bananas in your freezer and when the moment is right, whizz them up into One-ingredient ice cream (see p.139), using ground almonds, any smooth nut butter, chia seeds and ground pumpkin seeds as colourful toppings. Your guests won't believe their eyes!

The baby burger bar

• Mix up a double/triple batch of Mini slider burger patties (see p.111) and store in the fridge ready to cook when your guests arrive. Pre-prep trays of mini rolls of BB bread (see p.80).
• When it's burger time, grill/fry/BBQ your little slider burgers, ensuring they're cooked thoroughly. Bake your bread – it'll take 10–15 mins and you'll have lovely fresh burger buns.
• Set up a station for guests to build their own burgers. Create a production line with bowls of Baby guac (see p.72), grated Cheddar, diced fresh tomato and shredded lettuce. Grown-ups might like a dab of fiery mustard.

Other great party plates

Popcorn chicken *(see p.130)*

Magic fish fingers and crushy peas *(see p.107)* *freshly baked or reheated*

Jammy dodgers *(see p.155)*

Baby-friendly banana bread *(see p.150)* *served afternoon-tea-style with a cup of tea.*

Or any of the ***Mama treats*** *on the following pages* *(see p.171)*

New parenthood is a golden time, but let's be real, it's exhausting.

Mama treats: Nourish yourself

Did you think I'd forget about you? As if. Maternity leave can become a daily rollercoaster of caffeine and sugar as you counteract the tiredness of broken nights, breastfeeding or bottle-prepping/warming/washing, epic walks, baby-carrying, pram-lugging and all that extra laundry.

During my maternity leave I experimented with making healthy hacks on the kinds of treats I was craving from my local coffee and cake haunts. I shared a few batches with my mama-friends. Well, those chicks enjoyed them as much as I did. Now I regularly throw in parent-boosting, grown-up recipes on my online recipe-sharing feeds. These are some of the most popular, and easiest, I've ever dreamt up: nutrient-dense, unprocessed indulgences based on vegetables, fruit and unrefined natural ingredients. Nothing here requires much time or skill, and all are tried-and-tested crowd pleasers. These also work wonders on done-in dads and sweet-toothed toddlers or older kids (except the recipe with coffee in it!).

Magic chickpeas

Best known as the star player in hummus/curries (or in my Blender Blondies … see p.178), it turns out chickpeas are totally addictive toasted up as a crisp-alternative savoury snack. Why are chickpeas such a good thing for new parents to eat? Iron. Loads of us new mums are low on this. Even a slight deficiency can make you feel fatigued/weak/lightheaded/fuzzy-of-brain. I know, so far so all-in-a-day's parenting, but maybe upping your iron could help. Protein. Again, so many women don't eat enough. Fibre. Known to aid sluggish digestive function and act on the damaging type of cholesterol (LDL). Plus a host of helpful micronutrients. And they are very cheap, easy to find, and easy to stash in the cupboard. TWO kickass versions here, both on heavy rotation at our place.

MAKES 400G

WHAT DO I NEED?

1 × 400g can chickpeas, rinsed
2 tsp coconut or olive oil
generous pinches of sea salt and black pepper

Your choice of spices

2 tsp paprika
OR
1 tsp ground cumin and 1 tsp ground turmeric

WHAT DO I DO?

- Preheat the oven to 200°C/fan 180°C/Gas mark 6. Dry off your rinsed chickpeas by shaking them out onto kitchen paper/clean tea towel and giving them a rub. Tip them into a baking tray with the oil, seasoning and whichever spices you're using. Shake the tray gently to coat the chickpeas, then pop them into the oven for 25–30 minutes until crispy and toasted.
- Shake the tray a couple of times during cooking; be careful, these might spit and pop. Cool and serve.
- They'll keep for a week in a sealed jar, but it'll take everything you've got not to munch them up waaay quicker than that.

You-can't-be-serious raw chocolate fondant

The perfect naptime pick-me-up. Have you ever met a fondant pot that tastes good, needs no cooking and contains vitamins A, B1, B2, B3, B5, B6, B9, C, E and K, calcium, folate, potassium, iron, zinc, magnesium, copper, protein, dietary fibre, good plant fats, flavanoids with powerful antioxidant properties AND even a magic natural compound called tryptophan, which the body converts to serotonin – that famous happy-making brain neurotransmitter? Me neither. As if the chocolate hit wasn't enough, happy chemicals too? Nice one, raw chocolate fondant.

MAKES 1 FONDANT

WHAT DO I NEED?

1 ripe avocado
1 ripe banana
1 tbsp cocoa or 2 tsp cacao (cocoa's more potent and nutritionally punchy raw friend)
2–3 tsp honey (or swap for 2 soft dates, torn up, or vegan mamas can use maple/agave)

WHAT DO I DO?

- Put the avocado and banana into your blender. Add the cocoa or cacao and honey. Whizz for 20 seconds, checking all the ingredients have blended together well.
- Now shut yourself in a room immediately with the results.

Some great hacks

Add PB for Snickers vibes. Add desiccated coconut or coconut cream for Bounty vibes (whizz hard if using desiccated to break it down). Add maca powder for Malteaser vibes. Add vanilla for sweeter, more milk-choc vibes.

Instant raw brownies

Fancy a brownie? Me? Always. Well here's a secret – the best (and quickest and simplest and healthiest) brownies for MILES are sitting in your kitchen cupboard right now. And you can be eating them in 5 minutes. All you need is a bowl, a knife and a spoon – no weighing scales, no oven. Loaded with protein from the nuts and antioxidants from the cacao, one of these brownies provides quite a cocktail of essential minerals and plant fats. Eat two, and, well … you're practically superwoman.

MAKES 4 BROWNIES

WHAT DO I NEED?

3 Medjool dates, stones removed
3 tsp cacao/cocoa
3 tsp smooth nut butter (almond, peanut or cashew are all great)
6 tsp ground almonds
1 tsp vanilla extract
3 tsp cold water
2 tbsp honey (optional)
handful of chopped/sliced hazelnuts or almonds (optional)

WHAT DO I DO?

- Finely chop the dates until they're a sticky mess. Put them into a mixing bowl and add all the other ingredients. If you like a bitter, dark chocolate flavour to your brownies, you're done. If you prefer things a little sweeter, add the honey.
- Work the ingredients together firmly with a wooden spoon for a minute or two, then press into a small square dish/Tupperware container that's 10–12cm square. If you like nutty pieces, scatter the hazelnuts/almonds on top and gently press in.
- Put the dish in the fridge for 10 minutes, then get slicing. This amount makes four small, rich brownies. Double up for a bigger batch … and they also work as brownie cake balls.

Beauty-boosting chocolate-peanut bars

Close your eyes and you'll swear you're eating a Snickers bar. Open them and you'll be all "Hi every skin/hair/nail-supporting nutrient": vitamins, minerals, antioxidants, plant-based protein and healthy fats. Chocolate bars that make you beautiful? Don't mind if I do.

MAKES 25 BARS

WHAT DO I NEED?

Base
large handful of pecan nuts
9 Brazil nuts
6 tbsp peanut butter
6 tbsp ground almonds
9 dates, torn up

Layer
6 tbsp smooth/chunky peanut butter

Topping
2 heaped tbsp coconut oil
2 tbsp cacao/cocoa
2 tbsp honey
½ tsp vanilla extract

WHAT DO I DO?

- Add the pecans into a blender with the Brazil nuts, peanut butter, ground almonds and dates. Whizz your ingredients several times, in short blasts, to a thick paste. Spread into a clingfilm-lined dish/plastic container 15–25cm, pressing with the back of a spoon to create an even layer 1cm thick. Put into the freezer for a few minutes to chill while you prepare the topping.
- Melt the coconut oil in your smallest pan, then whisk in the cacao, honey and vanilla. Remove the base from the freezer. Spread a layer of peanut butter onto the base before pouring over the liquid chocolate. Return to the freezer to solidify for 20–30 minutes.
- Remove to a chopping board and slice (press down with a heavy non-serrated knife to make neat slices) into little bites or bars. They'll keep airtight in the fridge for a week.

You can swap the pecans or Brazils for whole almonds or macadamias, if you prefer, and swap the ground almonds for oats.

Blender blondies

Whoa. These are a game-changer. There's a bakery near me that makes the most incredible butterscotch blondies, and this is my homage. High in iron and calcium (two minerals very useful for new mothers), as well as slow-release carb, these treats contain no refined flour or sugar, and the only fat present are those naturally occurring in the nuts.

MAKES 16 BLONDIES

WHAT DO I NEED?

1 × 400g can chickpeas, rinsed
3 tbsp peanut butter
3 tbsp oats
4 tbsp honey
2 tsp vanilla extract
2 tsp ground cinnamon
pinch of sea salt
pinch of baking powder
2 tbsp cold water
10 whole almonds, sliced into slivers carefully with a large knife

WHAT DO I DO?

- Preheat the oven to 200°C/fan 180°C/Gas mark 6. Put everything but the almonds into a blender and whizz to create a stiff batter. If you're using a small blender you can do this in two batches. If your blender's having any trouble blending, add a splash or two more water.
- Tip the batter into a 20cm greased baking tin/dish, scatter over the sliced almonds, pressing lightly into the batter, and bake for 30 mins.
- When they're cooked the blondies will be squidgy with a cracked-looking surface. They'll become fudgy as they cool. Slice into little bites once cool.

Cinnamon and vanilla bring natural sweetness, but the star of the show is something unexpected: a can of chickpeas.

Index

H

I

J

K

L

M

N

Here is a quick reference guide to help you understand what your baby is eating:

GLUTEN-FREE

Huevos rancheros (Mexican eggs) p.49
Sunrise power baby protein bowl p.51
Baby shakshuka p.53
Pudding ... for breakfast p.54
Sweet potato toast with PB + J p.62
Baby hummus p.68
Baba-ganoush (and mama-ganoush) p.69
Baby guac with cucumber nachos p.72
Buildable baby frittatas p.73
Dunkin' doughnuts p.74
BB bread p.80
Tuna nicoise smash p.93
Buckwheat risotto p.94
No-roast chicken pot roast p.97
Baby bouillabaisse p.98
Gentle lentil dhal p.99
Baby burrito bowl p.100
Magic fish fingers + crushy peas p.107
Baby green curry p.108
Baby biryani p.112
Chilli con carne p.113
Brazilian baby jackets p.114
Magic pizza p.117
Provençal lentils p.118
Lamb kofta lollipops p.120
Mini Moroccan tagine p.125
Salmon fishcakes with tartare dip p.126
Popcorn chicken + rainbow root fries p.130
Malaysian coconut fish curry p.133
One-ingredient ice cream p.139
Paradise balls p.144
Raw carrot cake balls p.145
Raspberry ripple balls p.146
Chocolate truffles p.148
Baby-friendly banana bread p.150
Superbaby superjam p.152
Jammy Dodgers (with nothing dodgy) p.155
Chocolate fudgesicles p.157
Pina colada pops p.158
Dip-dye avocado pops p.159
Yoghurt bark p.160
Magic chickpeas p.173
Raw chocolate fondant p.174
Instant raw brownies p.175
Beauty-boosting chocolate-peanut bars p.177

NUT-FREE

Grandma's apple pie porridge p.43
Raspberry macaron porridge p.44
Baby bircher (overnight oats) p.48
Huevos rancheros (Mexican eggs) p.49
Baby shakshuka p.53
Tropical dream PJ pancakes p.59
Corn fritters p.64
Baba-ganoush (and mama-ganoush) p.69
Baby falafel p.70
Baby guac with cucumber nachos p.72
Buildable baby frittatas p.73
Homemade teething biscuits p.79
Stovetop flatbreads p.82
Oatcake crackers p.86
Courgette + cheese muffins p. 88
Tuna nicoise smash p.93
Buckwheat risotto p.94
No-roast chicken pot roast p.97
Baby bouillabaisse p.98
Gentle lentil dhal p.99
Baby burrito bowl p.100
Sardine ragu p.104
Baby green curry p.108
Baby biryani p.112
Chilli con carne p.113
Brazilian baby jackets p.114
Magic pizza p.117
Provençal lentils p.118
Lamb kofta lollipops p.120
Mini Moroccan tagine p.125
Salmon fishcakes with tartare dip p.126
Rainbow ragu p.129
Malaysian coconut fish curry p.133
Pho boodles p.135
One-ingredient ice cream p.139
Sweet potato cookies p.140
Blueberry muffins p.143
Baby-friendly banana bread p.150
Superbaby superjam p.152
Chocolate fudgesicles p.157
Pina colada pops p.158
Dip-dye avocado pops p.159
Yoghurt bark p.160
Happy 1st birthday cake p.166
Magic chickpeas p.173
Raw chocolate fondant p.174

DAIRY-FREE

Grandma's apple pie porridge p.43
Raspberry macaron porridge p.44
Cherry Bakewell smoothie bowl p.47
Baby shakshuka p.53
Pudding … for breakfast p.54
Tropical dream PJ pancakes p.59
Sweet potato toast with PB + J p.62
Baby hummus p.68
Baba-ganoush (and mama-ganoush) p.69
Baby guac with crunchy cucumber nachos p.72
Homemade teething biscuits p.79
BB bread p.80
Tuna nicoise smash p.93
No-roast chicken pot roast p.97
Baby bouillabaisse p.98
Baby green curry p.108
Provençal lentils p.118
Popcorn chicken + rainbow root fries p.130
Malaysian coconut fish curry p.133
Blueberry muffins p.143
Paradise balls p.144
Raw carrot cake balls p.145
Raspberry ripple balls p.146
Chocolate truffles p.148
Baby-friendly banana bread p.150
Superbaby superjam p.152
Jammy Dodgers (with nothing dodgy) p.155
Chocolate fudgesicles p.157
Pina colada pops p.158
Magic chickpeas p.173
You-can't-be-serious raw chocolate fondant p.174
Instant raw brownies p.175
Beauty-boosting chocolate-peanut bars p.177
Blender blondies p.178

VEGAN

Grandma's apple pie porridge p.43
Raspberry macaron porridge p.44
Cherry Bakewell smoothie bowl p.47
Pudding … for breakfast p.54
Sweet potato toast with PB + J p.62
Baby hummus p.68
Baba-ganoush (and mama-ganoush) p.69
Baby guac with cucumber nachos p.72
Homemade teething biscuits p.79
Blueberry muffins p.143
Paradise balls p.144
Raw carrot cake balls p.145
Raspberry ripple balls p.146
Chocolate truffles p.148
Superbaby superjam p.152
Jammy Dodgers (with nothing dodgy) p.155
Chocolate fudgesicles p.157
Pina colada pops p.158
Magic chickpeas p.173

ALL of the recipes are refined sugar free.

USEFUL WEBSITES + A FEW BOOKS

Allergy UK – www.allergyuk.org

British Nutrition Foundation – www.nutrition.org.uk

Jamie Oliver's 2010 TED Talk, *Teach Every Child About Food*. This sparked a lot of discussion at the time and kicked off all sort of great work on revolutionising how children eat in the U.K. and abroad. More than nine million people have watched it and it's well worth finding 20 mins for now your baby is old enough to eat. NICE – www.evidence.nhs.uk

The British Red Cross's video on how to spot and handle a food-choking situation in a weaning baby: *How to Save a Choking Baby*, available on YouTube.

The Ellyn Satter Institute – www.ellynsatterinstitute.org

World Health Organisation – www.who.int/en/

Bee Wilson, *First Bite: How We Learn To Eat*. If you like my recipes you'll love reading this book. A regular newspaper columnist as well as author of many books about modern food culture and food trends, you can also follow her on Twitter: @KitchenBee.

Michael Pollan, *In Defense of Food and Food Rules: An Eater's Manual*. No list of books on this subject would be complete without a couple of his. Pollan doesn't write specifically about baby food but what he has to say is very relevant to anyone tasked with feeding one. He's the guy who famously said "Don't eat anything your great grandmother wouldn't recognise as food". He's written loads of interesting stuff - most recently a book called *Cooked* about why he feels home cooking is the most important thing a person can do for their family's wellbeing. Find his talks on YouTube and follow him on Twitter: @MichaelPollan.

Joanna Blythman, *The Food Our Children Eat*. This award-winning British investigative journalist/mumboss knows a lot about the modern food system and isn't afraid to say what she thinks. This book is an examination of why and how modern 'kid food' has become synonymous with 'unhealthy food'. Follow her on Twitter @JoannaBlythman.

Niki Segnit, *The Flavour Thesaurus*. Gorgeous in every way. Breaking down which flavours go together and why, this book has inspired loads of unexpected flavour combinations in my kitchen. As we discussed in the opening of this book, it's a myth that babies need and like only bland, basic flavours. They can safely eat a range of foods, and this book will help make your baby cooking feel creative and interesting.

Bob Holmes, *Flavour: A User's Guide To Our Most Neglected Sense*. An in-depth read about the surprising ways humans experience taste and flavour written by a writer from *New Scientist*.

Isabelle de Solier, *Food and the Self*. About how in modern culture food has become much more than just stuff to eat – our food choices can define the moment we're in, change our mood, evoke memories of other places and times, and is an entire way of communication in itself – champagne means congratulations, buttered toast is comforting, remembering the way someone takes their tea shows you care.

Erlich and Genzlinger, *Super Nutrition for Babies*. A rather niche American text that's a bit old, and a bit extreme (lots of raw egg yolk and offal...ingredients I didn't fancy using myself and am not urging you to) but has at its core a simple and powerful emphasis on real, unprocessed food that I found eye-opening. It gave me confidence that my baby could safely eat more broadly than I thought.

Nicola Graimes, *Part-Time Vegetarian*. We eat all kinds of meat, fish and dairy in our house (respectfully raised/farmed and organic as much as we can) but I have a growing interest in the flexitarian life. This book taught me about cheap and versatile plant-based protein sources and how to make them feel like the main event rather than the side-dish.

Yotam Ottolenghi, *Jerusalem*. I've always loved him and think this book is his best yet. Baby B has eaten from this book many times and it inspired my recipes, including the tagine, hummus, baba-ganoush and flatbreads.